PRAISE FOR

Faith like My Father

"In *Faith like My Father*, John Fela delivers a heartfelt and powerful testimony that inspires readers to embrace resilience, grace, and unwavering trust in God. With honesty and deep conviction, he invites us into a journey of faith that is both personal and universally uplifting. This is a book that will strengthen hearts, encourage fathers, and remind us all of the transformative power of steadfast belief."

—DAVID HIRSCH, president of 21st Century Dads Foundation and host of the SFN *Dad To Dad Podcast*

"John Fela's memoir *Faith like My Father* is a raw, unflinching account of one man's journey through the trenches of special needs parenting, marital collapse, and ultimate spiritual redemption. What begins as a story about a father's seemingly worthless legacy—the repeated phrase 'Don't Panic'—becomes a profound meditation on faith, forgiveness, and the unexpected ways wisdom finds us.

Fela writes with remarkable honesty about his son, Chris's, diagnosis with PDD-NOS (now classified under autism spectrum disorder), pulling no punches about the exhaustion, financial strain, and marital tension that often accompany raising a child with significant disabilities. His candid descriptions of therapy schedules, school placement battles, and the isolation of special needs parenting will resonate deeply with families who have walked this path.

The book's greatest strength lies in its refusal to sanitize the experience. Fela doesn't present himself as a hero or martyr—instead, he shares his failures, frustrations, and moments of profound doubt. His journey from a 'New Age' spirituality through crisis to evangelical Christianity provides the book's narrative spine, though readers of all faith backgrounds (or none) will find value in his hard-won insights about perseverance and grace under pressure.

Particularly compelling are the author's reflections on disability ministry and advocacy work. His involvement with Joni and Friends and other organizations illuminates how serving others with disabilities can transform both the giver and receiver. The full-circle moment with his ex-wife' s wedding gift serves as a powerful testament to the possibility of forgiveness even in the aftermath of deep hurt.

For special needs parents, educators, and ministry leaders, *Faith like My Father* offers both validation and hope. Fela reminds us that our darkest moments can become the foundation for our greatest growth and that sometimes the wisdom we need most comes from the most unexpected sources—even from a father who seemed to have little to offer beyond two simple words."

—DOC HUNSLEY, executive director and
founder of SOAR Special Needs

"John Fela is a fellow special needs dad and friend who shares his remarkable journey of faith with beautiful transparency and honesty. His resilience and courage through difficult times are inspiring, and his story highlights the value of trusting God even in hardship. You will cheer as you see God do what he does so well . . . bring beauty from ashes when we 'Don't Panic' but learn to wait upon the Lord."

—STEVE CHATMAN, vice president of
Rising Above Ministries

"As a mother of a child with autism, I saw myself in these pages—in the fear, the frustration, the fierce love, and the relentless hope of John's story. John captures what so many of us know: that our childhood wounds often reawaken when raising children with challenges of their own. His story is honest, raw, and deeply relatable. It's not just a memoir—it's a mirror for those of us walking this journey, reminding us that we're not alone, that our past shapes us but doesn't define us, and that healing is possible—even when it's messy. This book is a gift to anyone walking a road they never thought they'd walk with the hope of restoration and redemption."

—SARAH BROADY, mother to a son with autism,
host of *A Special Hope* podcast, and writer at Hope in Autism

"In his short book, *Faith like My Father*, John Fela draws from his experiences growing up in working-class Chicago and the challenges he's faced in raising a son with a significant developmental disability while juggling the demands of work, marriage, and middle-class family life. The life lessons he has learned along the way regarding faith and friendship will inspire other dads with similar challenges as they chart a path toward a brighter and more hopeful future for themselves and their families."

—STEPHEN GRCEVICH, MD, president and founder of
Key Ministry, author of *Mental Health and the Church*

"We all have a story. But 'DON'T PANIC!' because John Fela shares his to encourage you in yours! From wounded to wonderful, bewildered to brave, exhausted to excited, inactivity to involvement, dark clouds to sunshine, defeated to directed, messes to miracles, wrecked to restored, crisis to Christ! John's journey encourages dads (and moms!) to welcome challenges, not panic, and take the next step of surrender to Jesus, joy, and the journey."

—DR. JOE and CINDI FERRINI, authors of
The Special Needs Parent: A Guide to the Life You Never Expected

"*Faith like My Father* is a compelling story of learning to trust God in the midst of hardship. John Fela takes the frustrating words of his father's mantra, 'Don't Panic,' and discovers in them an echo of Scripture's call to be anxious for nothing at a time in life he needed to hear it most! Through a broken marriage and divorce, the challenges of raising his son, Chris, and the surprise gift of love from his wife, Faith, John shows what it means to live out that hard-won lesson: 'Don't Panic!' God is near. His journey reminds us that faith is found in loving, enduring, and hoping through hardship, and in finding Faith, he found love, a partner in life, and a shared mission to serve other families with special needs children."

—REV. DAN HOLMES and REV. DR. STEPHANIE C. HOLMES, founders of Autism Spectrum Resources for Marriage & Family, LLC, authors of *Embracing the Autism Spectrum: Finding Hope & Joy Navigating the NeuroDiverse Family System* and *Uniquely Us: Gracefully Navigating the Maze of Neurodiverse Marriage*

"I'm thankful for the work God has done in John's life and through the ministry opportunities John has had. It's a hopeful story of forgiveness and redemption. Having children with profound disabilities can teach us so much about how our heavenly Father loves us, and I'm glad John is sharing those lessons with us through this book."

—SANDRA PEOPLES, Author, *Accessible Church: A Gospel-Centered Vision for Including People with Disabilities and Their Families*

A SPECIAL NEEDS DAD'S JOURNEY
OF FAITH AND REDEMPTION

Faith like My Father

JOHN FELA

Ballast Books, LLC
www.ballastbooks.com

Copyright © 2026 by John Fela

ISBN: 978-1-966786-67-2

Printed in the United States of America

Published by Ballast Books
www.ballastbooks.com

For more information, bulk orders, appearances, or speaking requests,
please email: info@ballastbooks.com

contents

To Chris,
my Party Monster always.

foreword

LIFE COMES AT US from many directions, often surprising, delighting, and disappointing us and sometimes delivering an overwhelming set of circumstances. We try our best to accept and understand the plan that God has laid out for us, but often, the question of "why?" is seemingly unanswerable—until we look inward to discover who we are and who we are destined to be. *Faith like My Father* is a leap forward in the process of that personal journey of discovery.

The author John Fela has dedicated his energy and made it his life's work to help bring understanding to not only those whom he serves but also to himself as he examines the challenges that have been set before him. As a son, a husband, and, more significantly a father, he shares his unique insights with a sense of compassion and empathy that comes from deep within his heart.

From the complex dynamics of human interaction to the beauty of embracing a son with special needs, John takes the reader through the emotions—the joyful moments and heartbreaking sorrows—of a parenthood that is different from that which was expected. These personal observations from the author illuminate a view from a perspective of reality that is built solidly upon a foundation of love, above all else.

As you absorb the words, you will discover the unconquerable spirit that underscores this fascinating and heartfelt narrative, offering a fresh insight into the complex world for those persons living directly and indirectly on the spectrum.

This is an entertaining as well as educational book that should be widely shared among all those who desire to get a glimpse into the true experience of parenting and loving a child of special needs. As you get to know the author, you will discover that this is far more than just a story about courage, commitment, and dedication, but rather it is an endearing story of unconditional love, an all-too-rare human condition.

—WAYNE P. MESSMER, *MEd, PhD, CSP*

We look before and after,
And pine for what is not:
Our sincerest laughter
With some pain is fraught;
Our sweetest songs are those
that tell of saddest thought.

—PERCY BYSSHE SHELLEY—

1 the family

TABLES. They define so much of our lives in ways both simple and profound. The kitchen table where meals are shared and budgets are discussed; the coffee table that a book club or small group meets around and where personal relationships share quiet, intimate moments; the card table that serves as a place for children's games and as space for the extra relatives at holiday time.

We had such a table in my home growing up, a dining room table that anchored the center of our house—we all congregated around it and used it for our own purposes. It served as a family meeting space, a spot where I worked on homework and played games on my very first ancient home computer system, and, of course, the center of parties or special events in our home. On a daily basis, however, it functioned as my father's personal space when he came from a long, hard day of work as a blue-collar truck driver. I would often gaze at him from the door of my bedroom, which, due to the smallish nature of our home, was situated right off the dining room and in clear view of the table. There he would sit, every night, at the well-crafted wood dining table, complete with its large, rounded, pillar-style legs with clawed feet. His favorite chair was at the head, obviously, and was significantly worn from not just all his sitting but also his reclining, as its well-shaped arms had repeatedly broken off because of too much stress in one direction.

The ritual he engaged in at the table was always the same: He would change into his favorite lounging robe after "washing up" from work, as he called it; put on his house slippers once his work boots came off; and open his familiar brown bag containing either a six-pack of beer or, in my later years, a cheap bottle of whiskey. His favorite glass, with the chunky bumps protruding out the sides, was always filled with ice, especially when he made highballs, and had the necessary long tablespoon to mix the concoction of ginger ale, ice, and whiskey sticking out of it. The stir of the ingredients in the glass would ring through the house like church bells, alerting my mother and me to the knowledge that he was now perched in his favorite spot. While he enjoyed his peace and quiet, it was not unlike me to come and visit, either intentionally or just because I became drawn into the orbit of his awareness as I would walk by. Sometimes he would even invite me to join him at the seat in the middle of the table directly across from him. Then, he would move into one of his usual soliloquies, filled with several of his trademark one-liners, the opening statement of which normally went something along the lines of, "My name is Teddy . . . and I'm an ACE."

This, of course, was his way of letting me, and anyone else who would listen, know that he was good, but not just good, the best. He was not shy about reminding the world on a constant basis of who he was and how good he was at anything he did. My reactions to him in the many moments we shared like this were predominantly those of humor. Because most of the time that I engaged him, he was, quite honestly, drunk, or getting very close to drunk. It was also pretty hard to take him seriously in those moments, as he would frequently trail off into some incoherent babble about himself, his past, or things that he could do, none of which were remotely believable in the moment. But there was one thing, one comment, one phrase, one trademark one-liner that he constantly repeated to me, whether drunk or sober—one that has stayed with me as his greatest legacy. It was really not much, just a simple two-word phrase, one that he almost always found a way to slip into any conversation: "Don't Panic." It didn't matter what the nature of the discussion was, where we were, or what might be going on, as my father had a very unique way of slipping it in regardless of the context. There's a fire and you have to escape a burning building? "Don't Panic." Get into a fight with a friend or loved one and not sure how to react? "Don't Panic." Stuck in a movie theater and a riot breaks out? "Don't Panic." I can still hear his voice delivering it to me in its overly rehearsed packaging: "No matter how tough things get, don't panic!"

I wish I could tell you that I loved my father for sharing that advice with me, that I saw the value in it and appreciated him sharing it with me, and that I felt I would be a better person for it. But that was not the case. As a young man growing up in my family, I had nothing but resentment for where and how I grew up. Seeing so many of my friends' upbringings and experiences with their families, specifically the boys and their fathers, I couldn't help but feel envy, wishing for the man who could've been my father but never was. I grew up learning to accept that my father was never going to be like the ones I grew up watching on TV or the ones I watched at school events or birthday parties. I was the kid who, instead, always wound up being embarrassed by my father in public, especially if he'd had a few drinks and acted in ways that made me emotionally shudder. For better or for worse, though, that was my father and the family I was born into, and my experience as an adult was shaped by them far more than I could imagine at the time.

IT RAINED THE DAY I WAS BORN. Then again, that's what it was supposed to do—any good Catholic knew that. It was Good Friday in 1974 when I came into the world late in the afternoon. I was the product of a very stereotypical blue-collar Polish Catholic family on the north side of Chicago. My father was a local truck driver for all his adult life, and my mother was a secretary for large and small companies in the city. They grew up in a Chicago that is all but forgotten, a major blue-collar city that was traditionally segregated. My family's ancestors settled in the neighborhood, the members of which were almost all Polish, in the early twentieth century. But almost as important as being Polish was being Catholic, as the major ethnic groups (Polish, Irish, Italian) all were, and they were also the ones who tended to be in the positions of power. Most notably on that list was the original Mayor Daley, whom my parents very much respected and who would regale me with stories about how he kept the city from being burned to the ground during the 1968 riots and also sounded the air raid sirens throughout the city when the White Sox, his favorite team, went to the World Series in 1959.

By the time I was born, the city's demographics were changing, and while most of my relatives had moved to other neighborhoods or out of the city entirely, my parents and a few other relatives remained behind. When my mother went into labor and it came time to go to the hospital, my father very respectfully drove my mother and dropped her off, then left. Since men weren't expected to stay with their wives at the hospital during labor and birth, he just left her, returning to work and passing along the sage advice of "Don't bring home the Easter Bunny," a bad attempt at Easter humor. My mother, of course, never felt there was anything wrong with it, as a husband staying with his wife, as I would do years later at the birth of my own son, just seemed confusing to her. What should have been a typical birth turned out to have complications—I was born with a club foot on my left leg. Although not as serious of an issue today, at the time, there was a strong debate over whether or not to operate or to allow me to just undergo years of physical therapy. The early years of my life involved being in a cast that ran the entirety of my leg, one that I repeatedly banged against the crib in the middle of the night. The cast was also a cause of rampant crying when it had to be replaced, as the orthopedist who cared for me had to regularly saw it off and reapply it as part of the therapy. My parents eventually didn't care for that physician's bedside manner and his strong desire to operate, and so they switched to another specialist who focused on the physical therapy side until I was about twelve. The dining room table I reminisced about earlier also served the purpose of an indoor track as I walked focused, intentional daily laps on my left heel around the table.

Despite all the challenges with my walking, I was a fairly normal child who lived a fairly normal life, and by the time I was four, I was healthy enough and ready to attend a local preschool. My earliest memory is walking into my grandma's house and announcing out loud that I was going to school. I can still feel the excitement I had going inside and sharing that fact, although my excitement for going to school would soon be tempered, as my only real memory of preschool was that I hated the lunches and would only eat at home. The trauma I experienced once I made it to kindergarten was a little more profound. My earliest memories from there include observing a fellow classmate bawling his eyes out and asking for his mommy. I was confused as to why he would do that, only to be doing it myself the very next day once I realized I was stuck in school for hours. Soon after that, I had an experience that has also stayed with me forever—this one regarding my struggle to learn in particular areas. It would only be years later, when I became a teacher myself, that I was able to undo a lot of my beliefs about my own ability to learn and understand.

It was the first week of school, and I recall sitting at a long, low table typical of a kindergarten class. I was at the table with another boy and girl, whose names I still recall and whom I would wind up attending school through eighth grade with. The teacher had written the first set of addition facts on the board with the number one at the beginning of each equation. She then instructed all of us to copy the ten equations onto our own paper—no other explanation, we just had to copy. Being the well-behaved young man that I was, I concentrated hard on doing the task at hand, focusing on the chalkboard halfway across the room and copying the set of equations very slowly. Having never done an activity like this before, I struggled to look at the board, remember what I had seen, and translate it to my own paper. I took my time, slowly writing each number very intentionally and making certain that I had no mistakes. I cradled my head in my hand as I got more tired with each pencil stroke. After what seemed like an eternity, I finished the task, mentally exhausted but relieved that it was over. I waited for the other boy at the table to finish, as the girl and I were already done. When all of us were finished, the girl at the table began to tease the other boy in typical kindergarten fashion: "I'm the first one, you're the second one, and he's the last one," resulting in that boy getting upset and crying for her to stop saying it.

What struck me the most about this experience wasn't how hard I had worked, nor how the girl had teased the other boy. Rather, it was the fact that I had absolutely no idea what I had written. I knew the teacher expected me to do it, and I knew it was something that the other students had to do as well, so I felt compelled to complete it. But I didn't know what it meant, I didn't know why I had written it, and I didn't know what I was supposed to learn. This kind of "math dyslexia" would haunt me for years. I found that I was definitely a gifted student when it came to speaking, reading, and writing. I was not a natural, however, at math, and I struggled to learn new concepts throughout all my years of school. My experience as a teacher later in life was the only thing that really helped me overcome it. I found I learned math much more easily when I had to teach it, and teaching also helped increase my confidence in trying to understand it. I didn't realize how much that experience would shape my life later, not just as a teacher but also as someone who would eventually work with special needs children and adults—and who would become a special needs parent. Everything about that experience—from the difficulty in doing the activity, to the teasing by the girl, to the failure to even understand what the numbers meant—allowed me to connect with my own child and the special needs community as a whole since I could identify with their struggles and pain.

Life for me in my early school years was somewhat of a mixed bag of blessings—there are definitely aspects of it I still look back at fondly and some that still hang over me with a dark cloud of emotions. I did fairly well in school the rest of my elementary years, as I loved school and loved learning. However, I was never very athletic or coordinated, so I was always that kid who got picked last in gym class and couldn't play sports and quite honestly didn't want to. Once the preadolescent years kicked in, I found to my horror that I also wasn't considered "cute boy" material by the girls. But I had friends and still got invited to parties and what we would call "playdates" in our modern lingo. Eventually,

I started to exercise more and style my hair and dress to impress, as they say, so some of those issues began to take care of themselves as I grew and became more confident.

Life at home was far more challenging and intense as I experienced the full dysfunctional behavior of my family and my parents' marriage. My father, who could certainly be described as a self-centered narcissist, could also be described as a flat-out angry drunk, and I saw this materialize in very dramatic ways. The man who could be a funny and jovial fellow one evening could shift gears and become an angry, bitter, and hateful man the next. Arguments were common in my home, usually revolving around my father's drinking. All were loud, some were physical, and some were just plain scary to a young child. My father never struck my mother, not that I recall seeing, but he was very aggressive with his language, initiating the yelling in their fights and matching or exceeding my mother's voice level. At the ripe age of seven, I would frequently yell at them to stop, which they mostly listened to, and sometimes I would physically intervene to break them up, stopping them from possible major injury. When it got to be too much, I did what I thought was a last resort and called the police, although I never got very far since my parents would notice me on the phone and stop whatever they were doing. Today, the simple action of picking up the phone and connecting with the police would be enough to motivate a physical visit to the home; however, in that place and time, the police would never show up unless it was considered a serious and real complaint. So all that ever happened was a call back by the police asking why they kept getting phone calls from this number, to which my mother talked them down and dismissed the calls as her son "just playing around."

The effect this had on me wasn't one of understanding or compassion—I was too young to process these events in any way other than pure visceral anger and rage fueled by my father's alcoholism. I didn't see a man who had a bad day here and there or was generally misunderstood. This was a man whom I repeatedly saw in his favorite chair with his favorite drink, day after day, with no change. This was not one of my friend's dads from school, the ones who would volunteer at the school events, or run athletic programs on school nights, or be present at church on Sundays with their family. This was a man who had, for all intents and purposes, given up on his life, getting himself up in the morning and forcing himself to go to work, then coming back and just collapsing into a stupor at the end of the day. This wasn't the man I wanted to be when I grew up. This was, rather, the man I didn't want to be. He was a clear lesson to me of what not to do as a husband and father.

My father's drinking also took a toll on his physical health. He came home from work one day escorted by a coworker, having experienced a very serious nosebleed that wasn't stopping by itself. I remember him walking into my grandma's house after work, where I was hanging out after school as I usually did while I waited for both my parents on weekdays. He was visibly shaken, and my mother and everyone else seemed fairly confused as to what was happening. We rushed him to the hospital, and he went straight to the emergency room. He was stabilized, and the nosebleed was temporarily stopped by the usage of a balloon that was inserted into his nostril, making his nose large and bulbous. He was eventually admitted that night for observation and spent the next couple of days in the hospital, later having the nose cauterized to stop the bleeding more permanently. For my part, I had a couple of nights where I didn't get much sleep and was very fearful of my dad's health. Although he was sent home, the nosebleeds continued, and he had to take extended time off work, which also meant more trips to the hospital; however, we had moved to a better hospital where all the family's doctors were and where I was born. Those doctors were equally baffled by the nature of the nosebleeds, essentially saying it was likely hemorrhaging due to high blood pressure and poor general health. Although he did his best to shift his habits and remain calm, the bleeding never stopped, and it was not uncommon for him to have wastebaskets full of bloody tissues and paper towels due to the extensive amount of bleeding he was experiencing.

One night, he had experienced so much blood loss that he was nearly unconscious, and although it was very late, after midnight at least, we never really slept well if he was having a rough night. When my mother noticed that he was not very responsive, she called the hospital immediately, and they instructed her to get him to the emergency room as quickly as possible. I was awake by this point and hurriedly got dressed, and we managed to get my father in the car and sped off on our way. My father was in the back seat with me as my mother navigated empty city streets, going way over the speed limit. He was clearly losing consciousness on our drive there, and my mother prompted me repeatedly to not let him fall asleep, that my job was to keep him awake. I talked to him and asked him basic questions like his name and where he lived, while my mother occasionally chimed in with heightened emotion. We made it to the hospital in what I can only describe as record time, and my father was readmitted for at least the third time. It was another late night at the hospital, waiting around to see if there was any word, and eventually we went home so I could get as much sleep as possible before school the next day. After another extended hospital stay, a bunch of bed rest, and a variety of treatments, including "highly encouraged" changes to my father's diet, the nosebleeds finally stopped.

But his health was a constant point of concern in our family, as he would experience a few years of no real issues only to manifest another large trauma at some point. He fell in an uncovered manhole when I was a teenager, which caused him to injure his leg and take extended time off work. By the time I was in college, he began to reap the effects of his traditionally bad diet. He had diverticulitis that he allowed to go untreated, refusing to even get a colonoscopy as part of a proactive health assessment. His experience with this condition proved to be almost as debilitating as the hemorrhaging; he began to suffer severe GI tract distress, resulting in him missing even more work and being up at all hours of the night because he couldn't get sufficiently comfortable. One day, it got to the point where he was doubled over in pain, and we went back to our "home" hospital to get him checked out. It was a Friday in June of 1995. I was off school for the summer and was getting ready to leave on a trip to Florida for a week with a friend. I went to the hospital with my mom to get my father checked in and examined by the doctors. The next day, I was supposed to get on the plane first thing, but I was concerned about the state of my father's health, especially since we didn't know what was going on. My mother assured me that it was fine to go on the trip, so I stayed with my father as long as I could that night, hoping and praying he would make it back home again. I wound up going on my trip, and my father wound up having surgery for his diverticulitis, which resulted in a portion of his large intestine being removed and required the usage of a colostomy bag for some time until he fully healed. He retired shortly after that since physically he could no longer keep up with the demands of the job. My mother continued to work, and my father occupied his time as much as he could, although I knew how difficult those years were going to be for him. He had no real hobbies except for watching TV and drinking, which he now had to monitor very carefully so as not to cause any further complications with his health. He stayed as busy as he could, visiting his friends at the bar even though he couldn't drink as much as them (although it never stopped him from drinking), driving my mom to and from the train so she could get to work and back safely, and taking a vested interest in me. I attended a college near downtown Chicago, and since it was close enough, I stayed at home for most of my time there, living in a "coach house" in the back of the main house I grew up in with a roommate. My father would offer to drive me places since I had no car for a time, ask if I needed anything from the store, share a meal with me, and see if I wanted to watch Michael Jordan and the Bulls in their prime with him. In many ways, I became closer with him in the last few years of his life than I had been for the over twenty years before that. It may not have made up for all the years I felt he was too drunk and checked out to spend intentional, meaningful time with me, but I could at least see he was making an effort, and I definitely appreciated it.

"JOHN, I'M SORRY, MAN. Your dad had a stroke."

The words cut right through me, and it seemed almost surreal hearing what essentially was a death sentence for my dad from my roommate, Chris. I was at my part-time job at a call center not far from both school and home, and after I'd received a text message on my pager to call home, I had dialed my coach house apartment's phone number and got the news. I clutched the wall phone in the break room tightly, half not believing what I'd heard and half wondering if it could have been prevented. After all, I had seen him earlier that morning before I went to school. Well, I didn't really see him. I stopped by my parents' house on the way to school, and my aunt, who lived upstairs, came down to check on him while my mom was working. He was on the bedroom floor, sitting up against the bed, and looked like he was half awake, but he was not speaking very coherently at all. I didn't know if something was wrong, but I knew I was late for class, and when my aunt asked if I thought she should call the doctor, I passively said, "Whatever you think," as I hurriedly went on my way out. After years of witnessing my dad drinking, falling asleep in his favorite chair, and being generally in a stupor, especially on the weekends, I'd just assumed the usual.

Now, he was lying in a hospital again, but this time, he was facing what eventually would become the proverbial final nail in the coffin. He had survived so much, so at the moment, I just assumed this was another hit

that he would just get up from. But this time was different. In the past, I'd felt as though I had no control over
his illnesses or the behaviors he indulged in that may
have caused them. This time, I could have done something different. I could have made the call to 911 to get
the ambulance there sooner. I could have gone to the
hospital with him to make sure he was taken care of. I
could have communicated with the hospital staff. Instead, I'd turned and walked away, because it was just
one more time, one more example of him paying for a
night of too much drinking when he knew better. To be
fair, he was under a lot of stress—not from work since
he was now retired but from cleaning out and packing
up my parents' home since they were in the process of
selling it. My parents had made a deal with a developer
to sell the property, and while they'd received a great
offer, they also had only a couple of months to pack and
sort over fifty years of accumulated stuff, much of it gar-
bage. He'd never handled stress or pressure well, and
with a major amount of work to finish on a deadline,
it had just become too much. I could have been more
tuned in to that, more empathetic to his situation and
state of mind, but I hadn't been, and for the first time, I
felt personal responsibility for his health.

While most people can recover and have a relatively
normal life following an event like a stroke, that was
not the case for my father. The severity of it and the
time that had elapsed before he actually got treatment,

compounded with his history of health issues, added up to him being just a shell of his former self. By the time I was able to visit him at the hospital, he was in a vegetative state, his mouth pushed to the side and slurring the little speech he was able to produce. He could not move his arms or legs without assistance, and even the simple physical therapy exercises he did seemed to make little difference. My interactions with him were not very deep—my mother and other relatives and friends were normally with me when I visited, and it was always too loud and busy to focus. But in those small, short moments, I was able to look into his face, make note of the few smiles he had when we put on a football game to watch, and stroke his hair lovingly because I had nothing to say. In many ways, I felt checked out because I wasn't sure if this was just another hospital stay or if it was maybe his last, and I was helpless to do anything now.

On January 1, 1999, I walked into my mother's kitchen after spending New Year's Eve at a friend's apartment. I immediately noticed my aunt with her head in her hands, and my mother turned to look at me while she was clearly bawling. Then the acknowledgement came: "John, Dad died!" I grabbed the closest counter to me and held on for dear life. The few seconds of shock that had instantly numbed my emotions wore off, then the bottom of my stomach dropped. I reached out for my mother and held her tight as we both cried and tried to console each other at the same time. She got a hold of herself long enough to explain what had happened. How she'd gone to visit him at the hospital, not realizing that he had already passed early in the morning and that she had missed the call from the doctor. She'd been there when he was still in the room, his body still warm to the touch, and she'd screamed for him to wake up. I wished on the one hand I'd been there to help support her and also to say good-bye to my father. At the same time, I thought about how difficult that would have been and that maybe it was a blessing and mercy that I didn't have to be there.

A few days later, just after a heavy blizzard hit the Chicago area, we had my father's funeral and said our last goodbyes. On the days in between his passing and funeral, I spent time with family and friends, which was helpful, but I also spent a fair share of time in private, mostly crying and reflecting on my father and the life I'd had with him. I certainly thought about many of the ways he'd failed as a father—and as a husband, for that matter. His drinking equated to him either not being present or having fairly violent mood swings where you never knew what his reaction to something would be. His alcoholism and bad habits aside, there were also many good times and memories, examples of him actually being kind and loving and someone who had the compassion and understanding of a true parent. In his tender moments, he could be a loving, caring man who made his best effort to connect with me, sharing some of his favorite foods with me that my mother would never touch, like smoked fish or a very pungent fried bologna sandwich. He would play with me when I was younger, running around the house or enjoying some of my favorite old TV shows in black and white with me. He would scratch my back when needed or rub my head lovingly when the mood struck him.

Beyond all this, I still wished he could have given me more, that he could have spent more time learning about the things I enjoyed or spent more time with the family as a whole, instead of running to the bar or bottle. I relished his sober moments because I got to see someone who was essentially a good man, but I always inevitably felt the letdown. On hard days, I almost wished that I belonged to another family, one without alcoholism, one without arguing or yelling, with a father who took pride in himself and showed real, intentional care of his family. I didn't understand why he was this way for a long time, but what I grew to realize was how wounded he actually was. He would share tales of dreams he had or talents he took pride in; however, every story eventually degraded into a state of disappointment or outright shame. It was clear that people in his life, including his own parents, had let him down on some level, and for better or for worse, he could never crawl out of that.

The ways he'd let me down still stood out, and as I reflected on what he'd left me—his legacy to me and what he'd passed on—I couldn't really come up with much. I believed he'd shown me how to talk to people and read their communication styles; given or, rather, forced a bunch of advice on driving to me since that was something he always took pride in; and taught me a few things about how to dress. More than anything, I kept coming back to those two famous words that he'd never let me forget: "Don't Panic!" I thought about how much I hated him for that, how he could have given me so much more, and how all I was left with was a catchphrase, one that virtually meant almost nothing to me. I may have hated him for that, but the reality is that I never really understood it, not until years later, when I realized what a precious gift it truly was.

I am different,
not less.

—DR. TEMPLE GRANDIN—

2 the birth

"JOHN, I THINK MY WATER BROKE."

Those were the words that woke me up out of a deep sleep in the early morning hours of December 8, 2007. I wasn't ready to hear those words, not yet, since it was about five weeks too early for them. We were still in those last few weeks before the expected delivery date, enjoying the "babymoon" period of living like a young couple without children. That very night, we stayed up late, had dinner, watched a movie, and went to bed without a second thought about our child coming early. Now, the possibility of being thrown into the next phase of our lives, both rapidly and unexpectedly, was difficult for me to process in the middle of that cold winter night. So I responded in a way that was absolutely nothing like the man, husband, or father I strived to be. The comment was purely motivated by selfishness and exhaustion. "Are you sure?" I managed to get out, half awake. "Maybe you just peed yourself?"

I received a confused and frustrated look from my wife, who kept her cool and said she was willing to wait to call the doctor. About ten minutes later, the stream of fluid still flowing, I was fully awake and agreed to let her call to get the doctor's advice. Sure enough, the suggestion was to start heading to the hospital, emphasizing that while we had time and there was no need to rush, we should get to the hospital soon. Since it was several weeks early, we had no bags packed, setting another piece of my OCD personality off. But we knew the time had essentially come, so we very calmly and purposefully packed our bags as best we could, got dressed, and jumped in the car to slowly begin our journey. It was now daylight on Saturday morning, and I very intentionally drove us down the local county road out of our development that connected to the larger state route that would take us to the highway. I made sure to be as intentional as possible as I made that slow, controlled drive en route to the hospital, wanting to be present and remember every moment of this day. I reflected on how we got there, the preparation and the training we did—both to become new parents and also to thrive as a young married couple. We placed so much focus on us being healthy, mature adults who were fully ready for this exact moment. The expectations for us as parents and the child we would raise were high, as so many people had poured into our lives from the beginning of our relationship.

I first met my wife, Emma, over five years earlier, in the spring of 2002. I had been invited by a close friend and his girlfriend to a woman's house in the north suburbs of Chicago. She hosted what were known as "drum circles." These were essentially groups of people who got together and played freestyle music with instruments, mostly hand drums and percussion. While the type of people who would normally attend something like this might be considered "hippies" or just eccentric, artsy folks, this was different. This event was in a lovely suburban home, attended by adults who were mostly twenty or thirty years my senior. Most were professionals, although many were in the counseling or social work fields, and all were New Age in their beliefs, which I very much fit into at the time. There were no drugs or alcohol allowed—rather, it was a potluck-style event, so the contribution of a food dish or item was appreciated, and everyone socialized around the table before and after drumming. Before the drumming portion, I stood at one end of the dining room table and glanced across the room at a young blonde-haired woman in a colorful tie-dye outfit who was busily stuffing a spinach wrap into her mouth. I took one look and knew that she was it. She apparently didn't know it at the time because when I talked to her before I left, I asked for her contact info, and she handed me a piece of paper with a very sloppily written email address. Needless to say, I could never figure out what she wrote, and so I never reached out, and we lost touch for several months. At the end of the year, I went back to the same house with my friend for the same type of event. I saw her again that night and got a real phone number that was written much more neatly, and the rest was history.

The reality is that the two of us should have never been together at all, let alone gotten engaged or married, since on paper we didn't make sense—we came from very different worlds. I was the product of a working-class, blue-collar, Polish Catholic home on the north side of Chicago. Emma was the adopted daughter of a wealthy Jewish family from the North Shore of Chicago. Because of the differences in the environments we grew up in, the resources we had available to us, and the overall differences in the cultures of our families, we should have never met. But for both of us, the cultural expectations of our families didn't really matter, both when it came to our lifestyles and also our spiritual beliefs. While we were raised in the religions of our respective households, neither of us really connected with them and actually had more of an affinity for the modern "secular spirituality." We rejected many of the conventions we were raised with, refusing to attend a church or temple and instead doing our own versions of prayer, meditation, and energy healing in the comfort of our friends' homes. It was this, and Emma's insistence that she didn't want or need her parents' money to make her happy, that prompted a very quick and whirlwind courtship. Despite her father passing unexpectedly just a few months before our wedding was to take place, we pressed on to the altar and were married in June of 2004.

Our wedding, and the first few years of our marriage, were very clearly a reflection of who we were, or wanted to be, in our new life together and individually. We canceled the fairly large wedding we had planned in Chicago and opted for a smaller "planned elopement" in Southern California near the beach and Disneyland, something Emma was very excited about. A small group of our mutual friends attended the event, and a friend of ours who lived in the area performed the service, getting ordained online just prior. Once we were married, we settled into the regular routines of a new marriage—working during the day, coming home for dinner each night, and spending time together on the weekends. We were both teachers, which meant that our lives were busy during the school year, while the summer allowed us to spend more time together. That formula changed for us when we decided I would go back to grad school a year after we were married. On the advice of friends, especially a "spiritual counselor" Emma was close with, I quit my regular teaching job to focus on getting my degree and would substitute teach while I finished. Normally, decisions like this would have motivated a couple to become more frugal; however, in our case, we did the one thing we shouldn't have: spend money we didn't have. We very much enjoyed going on several trips a year, and we also bought new cars and moved out of our townhouse to a much larger home with a big yard—on top of racking up more student loan debt. All of this, and now a baby on the way after having burned through a lot of savings and racking up some credit card debt. Most of our friends, especially one whom everyone always went to for advice, would always remind us it wasn't a big deal, that adults spent money and had debt. By the time we got pregnant, I was just wrapping up grad school, but I had not found another steady job in teaching. Nevertheless, here I was over three years after we'd first said our vows to each other, driving my wife and soon-to-be new baby boy to the delivery room. If I wasn't ready for this now, I never would be.

The moment we arrived at the hospital, it was clear there were going to be issues, starting with when we were first admitted and Emma was being checked by one of the nurses in triage. Emma had been battling a cold she'd picked up in the last couple of weeks, and because of that, the nurse suggested that she receive antibiotics from the IV they would give her. The problem, of course, was that we had planned for months to have a natural childbirth, specifically a water birth in a tub at the hospital. We had even sought out a holistic obstetrician/midwife who would perform the actual delivery.

Now, that part was all but done as the nurse counseled us on the fact that because of concerns over her being sick, we were looking at a traditional birth. By the time the afternoon hit, we had checked into our private birthing suite and had begun to prepare for what we didn't realize would be a long labor. I had also started to make the necessary phone calls to family and friends, and a couple of Emma's friends arrived to hang out and provide support while the doctor and various nurses came in and out. The message at that point was that we should be patient, as there was not much movement on our baby's part yet. However, the doctor told us that if there wasn't significant movement, we would be looking at the possibility of induced birth or a C-section.

The rest of the day and into the night was filled with pensive waiting as it became clearer that this would be a longer affair than we'd anticipated. Emma's two friends had stayed as long as they could, but they themselves had to leave to get back to their own families. At that point, I knew I would have to help Emma through the rest of the labor and delivery on my own, which I was ready for, although it had seemed as though at least one of her friends had concerns about that. I'd been heating up some takeout food in a microwave at the nurses station when her friend reminded me of how important it was for me to be present with Emma and how much she would need me. I bristled a little at her comments, thinking to myself that she didn't respect me as a husband or soon-to-be father, as if I wasn't up to the task at hand. Of course, her comments were only meant to emphasize how this was an emotional situation for Emma, who, having been adopted at birth, may have a hard time dealing with the experience of being a mother herself and may have a whole range of feelings linked to the experience of being abandoned by her birth mother. Yet I also couldn't help feeling a sense of frustration with her for making the comments, since, after all, I was her husband and someone who was always emotionally present, or so I believed. Wasn't I enough to handle whatever situation came our way given the kind of man I was? It was still too soon in my journey for me to realize that those feelings of inadequacy would show up again and again, way more intensely than I could have imagined.

Sunday came and went with little movement on the delivery front, and after multiple check-ins with nurses and the doctor, we got closer to the realization that we would have to try to induce labor with Pitocin. It was late in the evening when they began to administer it, and we made the decision with the understanding that it could bring an intense amount of pain for Emma as her contractions grew. We were also aware that we could request an epidural to relieve the pain related to the Pitocin, but that also meant Emma's contractions wouldn't come as regularly. Once the Pitocin was administered, her contractions grew and strengthened, as did the pain that she was experiencing. The expressions on her face quickly shifted from calm and peaceful to ones of excruciating pain and discomfort. The cycle of the contractions quickly became regular, and I could now tell when one had arrived by the writhing of her face and the tears streaming down it. It was at that moment, looking at her in pain, that I truly understood that I was the only one who could help her get through this, that this was the moment I had prepared for, the moment her friend had warned me about. I clutched Emma's hand tightly and said as loudly and clearly as I could to her, "I'm here, I'm with you," and "You're doing great." When I look back on our marriage, I have always considered this moment to be one of our strongest as a couple, with Emma showing her bravery in pushing through all her physical pain to deliver our child and me standing by her side. I didn't shrink. I didn't run. I was there with her for every step of it.

Regardless of how brave either of us was being, I knew we needed to get some relief as quickly as possible. Emma decided she needed the epidural but was in so much discomfort that she had trouble speaking, so I had to convince the nurses to administer it. In the middle of the night, she received it, and her body and emotions began to immediately relax, although there was still the actual childbirth to face. Luckily, the Pitocin did enough of the work to get the delivery back on track, and a couple of hours later, in the early morning of Monday, December 10, 2007, I stood in a now-crowded room while the doctor and staff surrounded Emma and the bed.

While I wanted to give them space to do their jobs, I also wasn't going to miss the moment my son came into the world, so I gently positioned myself in a space between a couple of the nurses where I could see the doctor's hands clearly. Our son was still being stubborn, so the doctor decided to perform a small episiotomy, or cut in the vaginal area, to help him to come through, and he did just that. Almost immediately afterward, and true to his nature, my son shot out like a cannonball into the world, crying and shocked by his new environment. He was very underweight at just four pounds, two ounces, but it was clear he had a healthy voice as he announced his arrival to the world that morning. Christopher Ryan Felageller, whose name was inspired by a dream about his naming Emma had had back in the summer, was born. We had the chance to briefly hold him before he was whisked away to an isolette in the NICU due to his low weight and to maintain his temperature. I stayed on one side of the suite while the nursing staff stitched and cleaned up Emma, and I briefly relaxed now that what I thought was the hard part was over.

A few months before the birth, we'd gone out with a couple we were friends with to help us go shopping for some baby items and have dinner. While Emma and the other wife went around the store looking at some different things and discussing options, I sat with the husband to have a father-to-father talk. The couple, who had two young kids, seemed to us to be a good model for new parents like us, and the husband had given me advice that would be quite prophetic: "Get your sleep now, get as much as you can, sleep until you're sick of sleep, because you won't get any later." That was my state the first week of my son's life, a week that was spent entirely at the hospital, sleeping on a couch in the maternity suite. We eventually moved to a smaller room that only had one small bed once we had been there a few days. Our routine was long, exhausting walks down the hallway from our room to the NICU every few hours to visit and do a feeding, which also became a challenge since Chris had difficulty latching during breastfeeding. He did enjoy breast milk and formula from a bottle and would even pucker his lips when he wanted more food. One of my real joys in those very early days was going to the NICU just to sit with him, which is all I could really do while he was in the isolette—sit next to him and just be. I still recall him lying inside of it, wrapped in a blanket with his hands perfectly clasped and resting on the middle of his chest. *Look at my son, the wise sage,* I thought, *lying there in such a peaceful meditative state.* I just knew he would turn out to be someone great and profound—he couldn't not be. I didn't know it then, but he would have an incredible influence on my life and affect me in ways I never could have imagined.

The end of the week finally came. We had stayed six nights in the hospital, sleeping in a new parents suite that barely fit one of us and technically only allowed one parent to stay there at a time. Each night, we played a game of stealth so we could both stay there until it was time to leave. On our final day, a doctor came into the room—not the obstetrician from the birth but a random pediatrician who was on call that morning—and reviewed our son's chart and basically said it was time to go. Chris had actually lost some weight and was down to just under four pounds, but after a week in the NICU and with no other complications, the doctor felt it was okay to go home, so we excitedly prepared to head out as a brand-new family. I went down to the parking garage, got in the car, and pulled it up to the entrance. After I helped Emma into the car and got Chris into the cradle for his car seat, away we went, feeling a sense of relief to be free from the hospital confines. Chris was doing much better, and we knew we could easily address any concerns about Chris's health. We had plenty of support waiting for us once we got home in the form of my mother-in-law, who had been involved in getting the nursery and house prepped for Chris's arrival, a couple of her friends, and some of Emma's friends, who, although they could be very opinionated, did really care about her and us. My own mother, of course, was included, too, although because of physical distance and her antiquated views on childbirth and child-rearing, we didn't see her much.

One interesting event that had taken place while we were still in the hospital occurred when my mother-in-law and mom came to see Chris for the first time. Emma's mom demonstrated love and appreciation for me for being by Emma's side through the whole labor. My mom, however, seemed befuddled and confused, wondering why I was present at the birth at all—my father wasn't there for my birth—but somehow she'd still managed to praise me.

Once home, we quickly learned that the child who had lain in the isolette peacefully and allowed me to quietly gaze upon him had vanished, replaced by a child who literally screamed almost every second, as if he had decided he wasn't cut out for this whole life on earth thing. We didn't know if this was typical behavior for a baby or if he was just "colicky," as his grandmother had insinuated, or if there was something else happening. Whatever it was, it made us rather jittery as new parents, especially during our first car trip to his pediatrician the week after we brought him home. The office was only about a ten-minute drive from our home, but it felt like nothing short of an eternity that day—Chris's screams in the confines of the car were almost unbearable.

"Sing to him!" Emma blurted out as we made our way down the road, to which I responded, "Sing what?"

"Anything! Just sing!" she exclaimed.

Backed into a corner, I busted into a ballad from my favorite band of all time, The Doors, the iconic classic rock group led by my adolescent hero, Jim Morrison. I loved their music, and I loved Morrison's writing—both his song lyrics and poetry—so if I was going to be forced to sing anything, it would be something from them. I opened my mouth, and in my untrained singing voice, I belted out the first few lyrics of "The Crystal Ship." Nothing, no change at all, and while it was a very short drive, I desperately switched to a couple of other songs, hoping Chris would like one, before we actually got to the doctor's office.

The pediatrician we chose was not our first choice. Honestly, we kind of picked her by default, mainly because we knew she supported a more "holistic" view of child-rearing, which, simply put for us, meant she was not going to overly push vaccines or an aggressive vaccine schedule. I want to say that we were not anti-vax parents, nor did we really do any research on the possible side effects on any level. We just knew from conversations with Emma's mom friends that it was better to take it slow. At the time, we regularly saw a chiropractor who had a couple of young kids, and she was very much into healthy, holistic living. Since we had developed a friendship with her, she'd suggested we check out the pediatrician for her own kids. After one meeting with him while Emma was still pregnant, we'd decided that he would not be a good choice, mainly because he was anti-circumcision, citing a variety of reasons why it was healthier to not perform that act. We'd known this about him going in and were willing to accept his position, although we'd known that we would circumcise our son for health reasons that other moms, some of them nurses, had shared and really just because we'd felt it was more normal, especially since Emma's family was Jewish. But this doctor wouldn't back down and made our initial meeting with him very uncomfortable, to the point that I'd not only told Emma that we should not work with him but also called the doctor's office to share with the receptionist how insulted we'd felt. That had been our first experience with having to lobby for our own beliefs on child-rearing to a doctor or specialist. It was certainly not the last time, but it definitely shook me, as I hadn't believed a professional could act that way with clients. So with him out of the picture, and since any pediatricians whom the obstetrician or hospital suggested were a little too far from where we lived, we went with a doctor who both Emma and I had seen individually as well. She was older but not too old, had good bedside manner, and communicated with us very directly—sometimes a little too directly, as we would soon learn.

One of the biggest struggles with Chris in the early days was his ability to breastfeed. He'd had difficulty latching from the beginning, and Emma had struggled to produce milk. Eventually, we just agreed that Emma would pump and we would bottle-feed Chris, but that still seemed to be an issue since Emma wasn't producing enough. That led us to switch to formula with an added supplement. The problem was that Chris was still not gaining weight and was labeled with "failure to thrive." However, we also soon experienced the difficulties of having multiple voices try to guide us. Friends of Emma just kept suggesting she eat meals full of protein and fat, but that never seemed to help. Meanwhile, the pediatrician and nurses at the office said that the supplements were essentially just sugar and not good for him. Things came to a head when the doctor made a comment during one of our checkups that Emma should be making breastfeeding and pumping her main focus instead of doing things like going out with her friends, which she had done in small bits in the first few months after Chris was born. This was certainly nothing I found concerning, but the doctor literally used the term "child neglect" with us. I thought this was rather harsh and told her as such, shocked that we had again found a pediatrician who would be so directly insulting to us.

We decided to leave her shortly thereafter, going with a recommendation from another mom for a pediatrician who was just as close to home but way more agreeable. Emma continued to pump for the first several months, but we mixed in formula and continued with the supplements. Chris began to gain weight, albeit slowly, but we were satisfied at the time. What absolutely stands out for me at this time in his life was just how exhausting it all was. I still fondly remember going to get bottles out of the fridge for a late-night or early-morning feeding and thinking I was getting ready for work instead and trying to make coffee. One morning, I was holding Chris in my arms and took a slip, sliding unceremoniously down our carpeted stairs and clutching Chris the whole time like a running back carrying the football across the goal line.

After a few months, life started to transition again, with Emma going back to teaching full-time after her maternity leave and me doing substitute teaching at the time. I was still hunting for a full-time position after getting my master's. Chris would be going to a friend of a friend who did in-home day care since we felt we'd rather go with someone we trusted than a traditional day care environment. The colicky behavior had stopped, and Chris's development at this time seemed to be as typical as we could have expected. He was generally a very happy baby, always smiling and excited to see people to the point that he would cry if he was put down when he knew visitors were in the house. He loved moving and would eagerly crawl around the house. I can still hear his excited breathing as he willed his body across the floor. Sometimes he would lie on his back on his jungle playmat grabbing on to a toy animal or rig and clutching it while looking at it intensely; I didn't know what this meant, but I was intrigued by his focus level. We had lots of support in the early days, with Emma's mom friends or her own mom coming by to visit and spend time with Chris, sometimes even letting the two of us get out of the house for a while. We wound up doing our own version of a bris for him a short time after he was born, not because we were raising him Jewish necessarily but because we just felt more comfortable doing the circumcision in the home. We essentially threw a welcome party for Chris and invited a bunch of friends and a small bit of family over, adding our own spiritual beliefs to the event since we defined ourselves as "New Agers" and couldn't just host a religious ceremony. We felt as solid and together as a family could, and in most ways, we lacked for nothing in those early days.

It was later in the spring and early summer after Chris was born that some dynamics began to change in our schedules and, more importantly, our parental roles. This laid the foundation for issues we would face in the next few years. While Emma had already gone back to teaching, she also decided to continue her side job as a real estate agent, which she'd started doing a couple of years earlier at the suggestion of a friend, whose husband was the manager of a branch of a large company in the area. Since real estate agents were mostly busy over the weekends, Emma was frequently out of the house, and that meant I cared for Chris most of the time. This was a role that I not only accepted but embraced with full force, considering the father I wanted to be—nothing like my own father, whom I could never imagine being as involved. My first big foray with Chris out in the world took place when he was about six months old and I decided to take him to a petting zoo and farm in our area that also had a restaurant on site. I vividly remember prepping myself for that excursion, loading the diaper bag that now lived in my car like I was packing for a week-long road trip. I had a bunch of packs of baby food, plastic baby spoons, bibs and burp cloths, and something that is still a favorite of his to this day, a thin receiving blanket that we called a "lovie." I put him in the car and off we went, deciding to stop first at the restaurant when we got there so we could both hopefully eat before walking around the grounds. It didn't take long for me to recognize how in over my head I was. I realized almost as soon as we were seated that I needed to go to the bathroom; however, I was now, for the first time, out with my son solo and couldn't just leave him. So I did the only thing I could think of: begged the waitress to watch him for a second so I could go, which she very kindly agreed to. I came back to a child who was once again demonstrating his penchant for screaming—being in a new and different place for mealtime was not comfortable—but I nonetheless plowed through and got us fed.

We spent many such weekends together, each time a different adventure—a new park or playground, museums in downtown Chicago, and forest preserves in the deep suburban green. I eventually got better at prepping and packing for Chris, and we truly had enjoyable days together, days I would not trade for anything. Most of all, I felt like I was not only nurturing my son but also healing myself, my wounded inner child whose father hadn't spent enough time with him, especially not the quality time I loved giving my son. Whereas my dad was always too tired to run and play with me, I climbed and went down every slide, crawled through every jungle gym and play place. I lovingly pushed the stroller down gently paved paths and went off-roading on bumpy forest trails, even when I was far too hot and sweaty—the huge grin I would get from him when he turned around was worth every second. But those first couple of years, as much as I treasured them, would not last, and the feelings of insulation from bigger problems, both in Chris's life and in our marriage and family, were just around the corner. I have always said that I learned more from my own father about what not to do when raising my own son, but my father would still prove to have made a significant mark on me.

Everything is going to work out—
there's no other option.

—KARI MILLER—

3 the diagnosis

A simple yet profound question, one easy enough to answer by most parents, but unfortunately quite difficult for us. It was at Chris's eighteen-month checkup that his then-pediatrician asked that question as part of a typical battery of developmental questions. By now, he should have been doing all the typical toddler babbling, repeating sounds and echoing what he heard in his environment. Chris, however, was doing none of this, save for some giggling and the occasional shriek when he was overjoyed. We shared this with the doctor, and her response was casual but clear: There might be a problem. Since this was our first child, and we didn't know any better, we timidly reacted with the obvious, "What should we do?" The question now asked, we anxiously waited for her answer, not realizing that the posing of this question, along with its answer, marked the beginning of a long and arduous road for our family. What came next was our introduction to the world of disability and special needs parenting, and although we had no idea of it yet, the path had been laid out right in front of us.

"You need to go across the street to the professional building of the hospital and make an appointment with the speech therapist. I don't know what they do, but they play with the kids and make them talk." We sat somewhat perplexed for a few moments, then shrugged and agreed. After all, what else could we do? We had been given what basically came down to bad news about our child, and as very involved, educated, and dedicated parents, we would do nothing less than our doctor prescribed. So we made an appointment, and a short time later, we took Chris to the speech therapist for the first time. This was the first experience we would have in a therapy environment, and we had no clue how familiar it would all become to us in the years to come. We entered a brightly colored room that appeared much like one of the preschool environments I had spent time in either as a teacher or as Chris's parent. A variety of bins with toys and sensory items were visible, as well as some things that were new to me, like what I would come to understand as a picture or visual schedule.

I sat in the room with the therapist, while Emma and her mom watched from the two-way mirror on the other side. The therapist was very friendly and loving and made an instant connection with Chris. The activities she engaged him in seemed simple enough. When seen through my early childhood education lens, they really involved a lot of basic tasks like identifying different toys or items and labeling others, then giving him simple choices and asking him to pick a given item.

Chris engaged with the items but clearly had a hard time understanding what was being asked of him, seemingly ignoring the therapist or becoming bored with the activity and seeking something else. While the first session could be chalked up to the therapist and the environment being new, there were a few more sessions that mirrored that one closely, and while Chris showed he could pick the correct item a couple of times, it was not consistent enough to show progress. At this point, the therapist basically communicated that there was probably a bigger issue here, and the next logical step was to get his hearing checked to see if that could be a problem. Due to Chris's age and communication issues, this test would not involve him responding to particular tones but would rather check the vibrations coming from the ears to see if they worked properly. The test was conducted, and his ears turned out fine, so we resigned ourselves to our next steps.

Something, however, also began to happen in our marriage and family at this point, in conjunction with our initial explorations of Chris's needs. We knew something was wrong, but we didn't know exactly what the best approach was, and in many ways, we believed that he might grow out of or just move past his challenges. Luckily for Chris, his family was invested in his well-being, but this was also where a divide began to grow between Emma and me, with Emma and her mom taking on the mantle of responsibility for Chris and his needs. They naturally worked well together and had essentially the same type A personalities—two very strong individuals who got quite a lot done. The bigger nature of those personalities could sometimes spill over and cause an equally large disagreement, but for the most part, I watched as they had very long conversations about where and how to find help and resources for Chris.

When I say I watched, I mean that my perspective was that of an onlooker. I was frequently left out of these conversations, mainly because I was watching Chris while they talked in person or over the phone, and I was normally filled in later by Emma. This was a dynamic I was settled with, at least for the moment, as I recognized Emma's natural gifts for researching and collecting information and saw similar skills in her mom. I allowed myself to just stand back. I would have appreciated an invite to be more involved, but I didn't want to push it, so my role in the family and the decision-making began to slowly shrink. I also felt a fair deal of shame in my own right, as I was only working part-time as a substitute teacher. This was great for our schedule, but I considered myself a failure for not providing.

Emma's mom eventually came back with information about early intervention services that were provided for free by the state since Chris was still under three. This would involve therapists coming to the home and evaluating him, then working with him in the areas of speech and developmental therapy. It was a great choice for us. Since I wasn't working full-time and Emma had stepped away from teaching to do real estate for a short time, we didn't have insurance coverage that would pay for anything beyond this for now.

Our life at that point consisted of Chris having therapists visit the house a few times a week to work with him on various skills and check in with us. We had tried placing him at a traditional preschool, but even in the toddler or two-year-old environment, his differences started to become more apparent, and his needs were a little more than the staff could address.

Eventually, we opted for a home-based day care that had fewer kids so he could get a lot more attention, although it probably wasn't the place he really needed to be. The mom who ran it frequently seemed overwhelmed, and because of the size of the home, her own family was always on top of the kids. It really felt like a loud, stressful space for Chris to be in, something we identified, but unfortunately, we didn't have much choice at that point. Chris also had regular fevers and severe cold/flu symptoms, causing us to frequently put him in the car in the middle of the night and rush him to the emergency room.

The drive from our home to the local hospital, though it was short, always felt like an eternity when we were as exhausted as we had become, and just as in the early days of his life, his screams cut through us. Due to our lack of good insurance, Emma went back to teaching part-time to get those needed benefits—and eventually went back full-time the following year—but this just increased the stress. In addition, I had finally landed a full-time job at a Montessori school, but it was a fairly long daily commute. Chris would unfortunately sometimes have to be at either the preschool or the home day care very late until one of us could get him. I remember how excited he was to see me pick him up, but my heart also broke every time I noticed that he was one of the last kids.

Because of all this accumulating stress and the atmosphere that our family found itself in, I began to feel a disconnect in our marriage and family. Our small circle of friends was mainly Emma's, her mom was still regularly involved in Chris's care—whether welcomed or not—and all our energy was poured into Chris. We rarely spent time together as a family, mostly taking turns being with Chris, whether it was me taking him to my mother's house or a museum on the weekends or Emma taking Chris to her mom's or her friends' houses when she had time. The days we were together were still enjoyable, and they frequently involved us going to the playground or taking the dog for a long walk in the neighborhood or at a local forest preserve. But I was still not very popular with Emma's mom or her friends—I wasn't taking care of the family in their eyes, and I was keenly aware of this. I was present and involved with my son, but that was not what my role was supposed to be. Like Emma's father and her friends' husbands, I had to be not just a breadwinner but something even further, making money hand over fist with no hiccups.

Emma had a friend who was a "spiritual counselor" and was the ringleader of this judgment. She hosted workshops and intensive life training for people from all over the country and often felt entitled to insert herself into our business. She was like a surrogate mom to Emma and would regularly check in with us, concerned about why we had created the life we had. She claimed to be a psychic, and for her, people created their reality, and if you created a bad reality, there was something wrong with your programming or the deeper intentions of your mind and heart. Usually, she would call to chastise one or both of us for our so-called "bad behavior," and her advice always involved doing a personal or intensive session with her. She was not cheap to work with—her hourly rate was a few hundred dollars, and a weekend workshop or program was several thousand a person. Emma trusted her completely and felt we needed her advice on everything, especially my career.

This would eventually contribute to our financial ruin, as our life became a vicious cycle of feeling the need to work with her to help us get our marriage and family back on track, then needing to figure out how we were going to pay for all her help in the first place. It did not help that the advice we were getting, specifically from Emma's friends and this counselor, was that "adults just have debt, you'll be okay," when they had many more resources than us. I was also beginning to feel the guilt and shame of not having a better job and not contributing more financially. It was truly a time in my life of walking on eggshells, trying to do the delicate dance of being present for my family while also trying to obtain better employment that would take care of them more. This was complicated by the bad advice we were getting from the spiritual counselor. If a job wasn't a "good fit" for me, there might be a call from the counselor or one of Emma's friends to suggest I needed to quit, even if I didn't have another job lined up. If I didn't quit, I wasn't listening to the good advice of people Emma trusted, but if I didn't work, I couldn't pay the bills. The simple questions of who I was or what my value to our family was were always weighing heavily on me, and I began to feel defeated as a man. My true solace, however, was my relationship with Chris. One thing I always loved doing was spending time with him, and I very much enjoyed our various adventures. Regardless of his disability, I treated him like any other child, and we did life together accordingly. If nothing else, I took pride in how I showed up as a father, and I felt the genuine love we shared together.

By the fall of 2010, things began to calm down a bit. I started my second year at the Montessori school I had been working at. I was comfortable in my role and enjoyed the students and the overall environment. Because of my relationship with one of the staff families who had a child with a learning disability, I was referred to a neuropsychologist their family had worked with and highly suggested for Chris. We traveled the relatively far distance to the office in the south Chicago suburbs and had the initial intake with the doctor, who had a very far-reaching reputation. She was kind and polite but very clinical in her approach, basically just asking for a narrative on our son and our experience with him. Then she communicated what the battery of tests would look like. We came back for several sessions over a few weeks, which included time with a variety of developmental therapists, then returned to meet with the doctor to get the results. The verdict was what we assumed, although not quite exactly. She shared that our son's diagnosis was something we had never heard of: PDD-NOS (Pervasive Developmental Disorder Not Otherwise Specified). It was explained to us that this was similar to autism, but it basically meant that while he had many of the markers for autism, some were not as profound, making PDD-NOS a more accurate label. The thing that made Chris stand out was his temperament. While he was certainly capable of screaming his lungs out when he was sick or uncomfortable, he nonetheless loved people. Because he didn't display outward signs of aggression or have regular meltdowns, he was actually quite easy to work with and be around.

The outcome of these results then led us into the next phase of our journey as parents of a child with a disability, as we now had to seek out clinicians to provide the therapies suggested by the doctor. In Chris's case, these were speech therapy, physical therapy (PT), occupational therapy (OT), and applied behavior analysis (ABA). He had already been getting speech therapy and OT since we'd started out with early intervention and some private therapies, but ABA was new to us and something that we would experience mixed success with.

Emma had gone back to teaching full-time, so we had better insurance to cover Chris's therapies, and his grandma contributed to whatever out-of-pocket expense was left over. The therapists we found turned out to be pretty spread out across the north Chicago suburbs. Some were closer to our home, but most were up to an hour drive based on the time of day and traffic. Our schedule, which we thought was already hectic, was suddenly jump-started to a whole new level. Between the two of us, we had to manage not only our work schedules but also all the therapy sessions, which happened every day except Sunday. Chris's pickup location changed based on the day and the particular schedule we were following given the season—sometimes at his home day care, sometimes at one of several therapy locations. The therapies also varied from more traditional, like speech, OT, and ABA, to more unique, like the equine (horse) therapy he'd actually started before he was three. Over time, we expanded these to swim therapy, music therapy, and even speech therapy in a pool because he was so motivated by being in and playing in water. The more therapies we researched and found, the more we tried. If something existed, we at least investigated it to see if it could benefit Chris.

After we had Chris's formal diagnosis, beyond exploring the various therapies, we also began to consider his school environment. We had concerns about the district we lived in at that time and what the future for him might hold once he was able to go to school. Emma had gone for a tour of the special education program that he would be plugged into, specifically a room geared toward students with autism. She came away from it feeling as though it wasn't good enough, and knowing her mom and teacher instincts, I agreed with her assessment. We explored some of our options, which unfortunately weren't many. I was working at a Montessori school at that time, so I was very knowledgeable about that community and had a feel for some of the different schools in our area and their overall culture. I loved the Montessori method because it made sense to me as an educator. It focused on practical life skills and motor development in the younger classrooms, then utilized some unique ways of teaching complex ideas in math and science as children grew. The actual philosophy of the approach had been invented by Dr. Maria Montessori, an Italian physician, in the late nineteenth century. She'd created a unique space to work with developmentally disabled kids. I was a real champion for the approach, so I brought it to Emma and suggested that we consider an environment like that for Chris. Because of my relationships, I could inquire with some people about Chris's education.

What I came up with was nothing short of a dream: a beautiful campus with a few different buildings for various age levels, nestled in a lovely wooded area on Chicago's North Shore. I knew the school from its reputation and also had a friend from my training program who had previously worked there, so I had a little bit of an in with the director.

I reached out and made a connection, and the director was very enthusiastic about helping us and bringing Chris on board and even took the time to personally give us a tour and answer all our questions. I remember just being in complete and utter awe while walking around the campus that day, reflecting on my own childhood as a city kid and the product of a neighborhood Catholic school. Now my son would be attending a very well-manicured private school in the middle of one of Chicago's most affluent suburbs. Of course, it wasn't something that we could necessarily afford, but that was where I was grateful for Emma's mom's help. We had a meeting with the special education staff and the director from our school district during which we essentially refused the services being offered to our son, and then we were off and running at the Montessori school. One of the key choices we made when Chris switched was starting him off in the toddler building, which, although he was technically a year too old for, was more developmentally correct for who Chris was.

The first year there turned out great, as the toddler environment suited Chris's needs perfectly. Under the Montessori approach, unlike a traditional preschool, the classroom is designed to help facilitate fine and gross motor development. Many of the items in Chris's room were similar to what I had seen in many of his therapy rooms, specifically PT, like balance beams and rails. There was not as much focus on writing or drawing per se, but there was a focus on building the fine motor skills to hold a pencil or marker. This included picking up and manipulating shapes with knobs on them, like puzzle pieces, using a pencil grip.

By the time the fall rolled around, however, we began to run into some problems when Chris was moved into the primary classroom designed for three- to six-year-olds. While Chris starting a year late was not the issue, the support that Chris needed had become glaringly evident, and unfortunately, the lead teacher was not accommodating to his needs. The teacher was classically trained in the European Montessori model as opposed to the more Americanized model that I had been trained in. That meant that she was not willing to adjust the classroom to support him because the structure of the environment was such that there couldn't be significant changes or accommodations made for a student—everything had its place. Although there were a couple of aides in the classroom who did support and direct Chris as best they could, they were still not there to work specifically with him. Since he didn't have the cognitive skills to follow directions well, he mostly floated around the space.

We eventually recognized this, and in order to get him more direct support, we asked his ABA clinic to send a therapist to school with him who could shadow him and help him pick up on the classroom expectations and materials. The other problem we now encountered, though, was that this therapist was not familiar with Montessori. The environment seemed strange and confusing to her, and the teacher was not going out of her way to help her acclimate.

So the whole situation became an "oil and water" scenario, and we quickly realized that we needed a new placement for him. This would not be an easy decision for us, as we knew that he couldn't go to a traditional preschool but didn't like the option of our home school district. What cemented our decision was something that no parent ever wants to hear or experience for their child. We received some reports from the ABA therapist, who, as part of her time with him, would accompany the class to the playground. The therapist had observed that while on the playground, the teacher was telling the other students not to play with our son and was keeping them from him. While this may not make sense to most parents, I knew because of my Montessori background that this teacher, who was so attached to her environment being perfect and orderly, was keeping my son and his "bad behavior" away from them.

Needless to say, we were livid, so we began to explore other options. We decided our best choice would be to sell our home and move to a community with a better public school district, but we would keep him at his current school until the end of the school year. After we had an opportunity to sit down and discuss our concerns with the director and the teacher, they did become more engaged with Chris, but the damage had been done, and we stated as much.

The choice to sell our home and move was, on the one hand, an easy one, but on the other, one more layer of stress during an already stressful time for our family. It only added on to the feelings of inferiority and failure I had about my role. This was just the beginning of one of the most challenging seasons of my life for many reasons, none of which I felt I had any control over and none that I really had any answers for. As things escalated, I quite literally thought this would be the end of me and my family altogether, and there was nothing left that could save me.

I have said these things to you,
that in me you may have peace.
In the world you will have tribulation.
But take heart; I have overcome the world.

—(JOHN 16:33 ESV)—

4 the collapse

"I CAN'T DO THIS ANYMORE."

That was one line I never wanted to hear, but there it was, hanging in the air in the middle of the car as Emma drove and I sat dumbfounded and grieving silently in the passenger seat. I thought this conversation could only end in tragedy—the end of my marriage and my family. The whole day, of course, couldn't have been any worse, and it was also the culmination of several months of extreme hardship we'd faced from the beginning of the year. It was April of 2012, and our family had experienced a very dramatic downward spiral since right around January after the incident at Chris's school, getting progressively worse up to this day. I sat in utmost defeat, pondering where everything had gone wrong. How did I get here? How did things become this bad? I had lost my full-time teaching job earlier in the year and was stuck working part-time jobs to help support us, though we were barely scraping by. Our marriage and relationship had suffered mightily, and there was so much stress and tension in our home that even having a small amount of time for ourselves was barely thinkable. Chris's school situation was still tenuous, and now, Emma was suffering from some potentially serious health issues with her heart. She'd begun to feel fatigued, and her doctor had recommended getting a CT scan.

As we drove, she laid out all the reasons why our marriage wasn't working. It was mostly my fault. She was already surrendering the marriage. "You can take the Easter ham we got and bring it to your mom if you want," she said. We were coming back from an appointment at a hospital on the north side of the city, an area I was pretty familiar with since it was a hospital near my mom's house that my aunt had stayed at several years before. One of the streets we drove on was also one where my uncle used to live as a child, and we even drove past his house on the way home. I reflected on the days I would spend there as a kid when my parents would visit, and I spied the day care center that was right next door to the house. They had what I'd considered at the time to be the coolest playground I had ever seen, and my family would let me jump over the short cyclone fence in the yard to play with a couple of other kids from the neighborhood. What would that young man think of where and who

I was now? I was saddened to the point that I wished I could just walk out of the car and into the past, to that place, where all I had to care about was playing tag and getting a random popsicle in the summer. Instead, I was now hearing Emma talk about how this year for Easter, I would possibly be going to my mom's alone, without my wife and child, and have to explain how life had completely destroyed me.

The year had started out somewhat ominously, with a perceived dark cloud coming in to hang over us, the first signs of which had come from my teaching job. I had accepted an offer with a new Montessori school that I thought would be a great fit. I had several interviews and conversations with the director and founder, all very positive. I was then given a solid offer—more than I was making at my previous job and on par with what my level of education would command. The school was, unfortunately, about a ninety-minute drive each way, which sounds extreme, but I had driven over an hour to my previous school, and since the offer was strong enough, I decided to suck it up and deal with the longer commute.

While the school year started okay, I gradually noticed that the director started to become more demanding and ask very specific questions about how I was running my classroom. She also chastised me for relatively minor issues or offenses and requested regular meetings.

Eventually, the administration started having sit-downs with me and drafted formal letters of complaint about my performance. I was asked to improve on those until the issues were rectified. In a healthy environment, this would have been a way to develop an employee positively with constructive criticism, but it was clear to me after a while that they were simply covering up their intentions. By the time the end of December came, they asked me to resign, which I could have fought, but I was just frustrated and exhausted, so I agreed to be phased out of my position over a few weeks.

Once I left my job, I was desperate to find work, picking up anything I could in terms of part-time or temporary work. I could have easily gone back to substitute teaching; however, Emma didn't like the idea of me going back to that, so I grabbed what I could while I applied for jobs. The first thing I picked up was a job as a personal care worker with a family in the north Chicago burbs. I would be caring for an adolescent boy with cerebral palsy who was also a wheelchair user. While I had plenty of hands-on experience with Chris, I was not familiar with many other disabilities at that time, and other than being a substitute in special education environments, I hadn't been around many disabled people. I met with the parents, who were very sweet, loving people; the mom was a gym teacher at a local high school, and the dad chose to stay at home so that he could support their son with disability and his able-bodied brother. I explained that I didn't know a whole lot about doing this kind of support, but the parents insisted that it was very easy and that I could just shadow and watch the dad in the beginning—ultimately, they said, it was about just spending time with him.

I worked there a few days a week, mostly in the afternoons and evenings, doing a variety of tasks like feeding him, changing his diaper, and helping him get prepped for bed, with lots of TV shows in between. While I worked for them, I continued to job search, and I gradually became more and more frustrated with myself and the situation. I realized that I could not continue to just work in this role for a few hours a week and checked my phone when possible to look at potential job listings. One night, I was changing the young man's diaper on the floor. I remember kneeling on his bedroom floor and, while in the act of wiping him, saying in my mind, *God, I'll do this for every person in the world if it means I can keep my family.*

I eventually moved on to a few other short-term gigs, some in retail and some for small offices, none of which I could support myself with, let alone my family. I continued to try to find teaching jobs. That was especially challenging at that point because it was already halfway through the school year, and other than substitute jobs, which Emma didn't want me to do, the only other choices were jobs in preschools or Montessori schools, but I had little success there as well. One of the jobs I took was for a marketing company, passing out samples in major big box retail stores. This was a horrible experience for many reasons, but on that particular day in April, I was on my way to a store to set up for the day when my car, which was now about eight years old and had suffered months and months of long commutes, decided to not start anymore. I was able to get it to a local mechanic, but they were extremely busy and took hours to even look at it, so I was stranded at the garage, completely powerless. The last thing I wanted to do that day was call Emma since I knew she was going to a doctor's appointment that she was already very anxious and concerned about, but I had no choice. I called her while she was on her way to the hospital and explained my situation, and her response, while supportive, was nonetheless peppered with frustration. I practically begged for her to just pick me up so I wasn't stranded there, and finally, by the early afternoon she was able to pick me up on her way to the appointment. Since it had forced her out of her way, we barely made it to the hospital in time. I sat and waited for the scan to be done, now feeling completely wrecked—not only was I without a car, but I had also nearly made her late, and she was clearly overwhelmed.

When she finished, we went back to the car, and as we drove away, she bared her feelings without stopping, and I felt my very soul being put through a ringer for almost the next hour. She said she couldn't do this anymore. How did we even get here, and whose fault was it anyway? Was it my fault? Sure, how could it not be? I obviously had not honored my commitment to my marriage and family—what kind of man lets his career tank so badly, anyway, and can't manage to hold even a basic teaching job? Was it Emma's fault? She certainly played a part, being someone who grew up in a relatively affluent family. She wanted to live the life of her parents and the friends she idolized, the ones who reminded us that spending and debt were no big deal. Was it other people's fault? Certainly could be, as her friends controlled a lot of the choices she made, especially the spiritual counselor, whose advice Emma always took and, therefore, made me take. Emma's mom was also very involved, and while she could be very generous and supportive, she could also be very demanding and had no issue giving us advice about anything regarding our family to the point where she seemed like more of the husband in the house than I did.

The car finally made it to our development, and Emma turned onto the main road, pulling over next to the pond and small park that was near the entrance. She had intended to "go over our story," as far as what she wanted to share with her mom once we got back home. I couldn't handle it anymore. I didn't go to a place of rage or anger—I went the complete opposite way. I broke down and cried like a baby, no filter, just let it all go. "I don't want this!" I stammered out between sobs, trying to reason my way out of an unreasonable situation. I was able to get out a few other lines about how much I was hurting because I was hurting Emma and Chris so much. Finally, I spewed out how I couldn't lose my family, and I would do anything to stop it from happening. Emma fell silent for a few moments, her voice and body language softening, naturally responding to me clearly being in pain. "Okay," she said in a now calm and more settled voice. "Let's talk more later, but I won't say anything to her now." With that, we returned home.

The same pattern that had been going on for the last few months continued into the summer, with me juggling different jobs and Emma finishing up her school year, as well as her teaching ESL classes at the local community college. I applied for several jobs as both a teacher and administrator at some preschools and Montessori schools, most of which fell through, until I finally landed a teaching job at a preschool in Wisconsin, just outside of Milwaukee. While this was not necessarily close to us, it was actually a shorter commute than the one I had been doing at my previous school, and at least it was steady work. Our family situation was barely treading water, and it was clear that Emma really didn't want to spend a lot of time around me or as a family, almost as if she was consciously preparing for a separation. A few of her friends were also in the middle of a separation or divorce, and it almost seemed like they were creating their own divorced wives club or something. I spent a lot of time with Chris by myself, just as I had done when he was first born but even more so now, taking him out on weekends or going to visit my mother. The whole time, I started to condition myself for what felt like our inevitable demise.

Because we lacked any real objective support in terms of our family and situation, whatever advice we received came from Emma's friends or the spiritual counselor, and as time went on, it became more and more extreme. At one point in the spring, after the meltdown in the car happened, the counselor made a recommendation that since our situation was created largely by me, intentionally or unintentionally, she felt that I needed to be presented with an ultimatum. The ultimatum was as follows: I needed to find a job that paid at least a $50,000 a year salary by July 1, or I would be kicked out of the house. Her reasoning was that if I couldn't "manifest" a job on that level, I wasn't really willing to contribute to the family. That was not an easy thing to accomplish, especially given the situation I found myself in, as my only real way to make that happen was to get a new teaching job, which wouldn't come available until the fall. The job I had gotten near Milwaukee certainly didn't qualify, and moving into a whole new field, which some people had suggested to me, was as daunting a task as well. I was running out of choices and hope. At one point, I sat down in front of my computer, fearing that I would be thrown out with no way to take care of myself, much less my family. I wrote three letters, one to Chris, one to my mother, and one to Emma—all of them suicide notes. I told myself I wouldn't go ahead with anything until I knew I was totally out of choices, which, luckily, I still had, but just barely.

The thing that really hit me during all of this was the fact that I really had no one to talk to who was truly in my corner. I was concerned that we had no one trying to save our marriage in general, but personally, I felt completely on an island. When things had started to disintegrate, Emma had suggested talking to a therapist to help me sort some things out for myself and consider how I was approaching my situation. He was a nice enough man, but he really just repeated things I said and engaged in small talk—a very surface-level type of therapy, which was absolutely not what I needed. After a couple of months, I decided to quit seeing him, but, still feeling that we needed some real therapy in our lives, I began to communicate with a marriage counselor whom one of Emma's friends had recommended. Emma had basically given me the responsibility to set everything up, and I sensed a lot of it was her just ready to give up on us. After several weeks of trying to connect with her, I was finally able to get something scheduled, and we both agreed to move forward. We began seeing her in the early summer. By that point, things were probably at their worst, and the July 1 deadline was looming. But it was the start of real, serious therapy for our marriage, something we had been sorely missing.

Regardless of finding a solid therapist for once, I still felt the need to reach out to other guys for some support and guidance. One of the things I felt I could lean into was the men's group at the church we were attending. It was a Unitarian church about a half hour south of us, one that we were both comfortable and familiar with. We had actually thought about hosting our wedding there and had agreed that it fit our particular set of beliefs at that time. Essentially what I would later refer to as "church for atheists," it consisted of a very interesting amalgamation of beliefs and backgrounds. Its focus was more on community and God in the universal sense—no saviors, no judgment, no condemnation, just people trying to live and do their best. We'd started attending the previous fall and had immediately felt welcomed by the congregation and made some friends with families our age. One of the things they offered was a men's group, which met weekly on Friday evenings, and I had been attending off and on for several months. One evening in early summer, I went to the group like usual, but this time, I decided to really open up about what was going on to them. Feeling like they would be understanding and supportive, especially since they were on average twenty years older than me, I thought it would be a wise thing to do.

Right before I went into the meeting that night, I sat in my car in the parking lot since I'd arrived about a half an hour early. I felt like I should do something productive with the extra time I had, so I decided to call a couple of my oldest friends. One was my best friend from high school, Ed, and the other was my roommate in college,

Chris. Both of them were married but didn't have kids yet, certainly not any with disabilities. Because I'd known them as long as I had and trusted them over most people I knew, I tried giving them a call. I felt a certain amount of anxiety having to speak to them about everything that was happening, and in many ways, I didn't even know if they would believe me or not. But they were both understanding and supportive, although they were confused and didn't really seem to grasp how things had gotten so out of control. Ed, who had consistently been one of my closest friends since our freshman year in high school, was honest but direct, as always. "What exactly is going on with your kid? What's wrong with him?" I shared all the struggles with his development—the non-speaking and the difficulty of finding a school that served him— on top of the financial and marital issues that had come up more recently. "I don't know what to tell you, man, but I'm just gonna be honest. A lot of this doesn't seem fair to you, and if it were me, I would just walk away." On one level, he was absolutely right—a lot of this didn't seem fair to me at all—but a lot of it was mine to deal with, and regardless of how it balanced out, there was no way I could leave my family. "Well, just take care of yourself, bro, and make sure you let me know how you're doing." The call with Chris was pretty similar, his biggest piece of comfort being "I know it's not easy, it never is." I came away from both conversations feeling despondent, but at least I knew there were people from my past who would be there.

I stepped out of the car and went into the church for the meeting. We usually met in a few different places in the building; this time, it was a meeting room with couches and a table in the middle that had some bags of chips and soft drinks. I greeted the fairly regular group of guys, about twelve of them total, and reclined on the sofa as we went around the room sharing updates about our various lives. When my turn came up, I decided to go for it—I had nothing to lose, and I needed to get some positive news from somewhere. I laid it all out: everything that was going on, everything with Chris, everything with my marriage to Emma, everything with my job and financial struggles, the whole pile of mess. When I finished, I sat quietly and just waited for a response, assuming there would be a whole flurry of comments and questions from everyone. Instead, there was nothing, not a darn thing. They sat in silence for what felt like a couple of minutes, though it was probably shorter than that.

Finally, the group leader, who was a nice enough guy, spoke up. "Wow, that's really tough. I'm sorry to hear that. But what you need to know is that it's going to be okay." What? That was it? It was going to be okay? That was not what I wanted or needed to hear. I wanted compassion, a pat on the back or, dare I say, an actual hug. Instead, no one moved or flinched. No one got out of their seat and approached me. I simply sat mired in confusion and disappointment. I wished these guys could have been different, more charitable with their responses, but maybe that just wasn't who they were. I had to let it go and hope, somehow, that a space would open for the guys I needed to connect with to show up.

I walked out of the church building back to my car and drove home. I was a defeated man, with no one to listen to or hear me, no one who understood what I was going through, no one with compassion for my situation. I didn't just need a new group of guys—I needed a miracle.

Friendship is born at the moment
when one person says to another,
"What! You too? I thought that I was the only one."

—C.S. LEWIS—

5 the rescue

"LORD, I LIFT UP JOHN in prayer to you."

What? Did I really just hear that guy say that? The guy's name was Matt, a man I had never met before now and so far had only known for a couple of hours while attending this new men's group. This was a group that I had been introduced to by a coworker of Emma's who attended the church that hosted it. Specifically, it was a men's Bible study that met on Wednesday nights—a group that I had been encouraged by Emma to join after she had spoken to her friend about her church and if it offered something for guys. Of course, being "encouraged" more so resembled Emma's overall frustration with the state of our lives and marriage. I was grasping for straws and would try to do anything to keep my family, so when it came up, I jumped on the opportunity and reached out to the assistant pastor. We played a few days of phone tag before finally connecting while he was at the hospital with his son, who was being treated in the ER for a minor injury. He didn't have much time to talk but listened to my story for a few minutes and just suggested I try it.

The church was about a fifteen-minute drive from my home—not a megachurch but definitely not small—nestled in a very pleasant neighboring suburb. I pulled into the parking lot and made my way to the side door I'd been instructed to go in, my head swirling with questions and concerns during my short walk. What were *these* guys going to be like? I hoped that it would be a helpful experience, but would I really fit in with real church guys who actually met on their own for Bible study? My perception of church culture, especially conservative evangelical church culture, was not an inviting one. I considered what would happen if the conversation went in a direction I didn't understand or couldn't relate to. The church building itself was definitely different from places I had been in the past, totally opposite from the Catholic churches I'd attended as a child. It was sort of like the church we had just come from, not truly modern but also not suggesting a church. I walked into the side door and entered what was actually the young adult portion of the building; the guys met in their worship space. They were clearing out the center of the room and making a big circle of folding chairs. The various music instruments and mixing boards reminded me of many a studio I had hung out at with my musician friends back in my teens and twenties. I grabbed a seat right in the middle of the circle, and guys slowly wandered in and filled up the space, a few coming up to greet me before the discussion started. I was asked to give a brief intro to the group, which I kept short since I was new and unsure.

The assistant pastor I'd spoken to on the phone opened the group up, and while he was friendly and welcoming, he also made it clear that they "hold the Bible up high" in the group, which was an indirect way of saying this was a Christian group for Christian guys. The group felt both very new and very familiar at the same time. For the first time since elementary school, I actually cracked a Bible open and read along with the scripture passage. I was comfortable with the discussion since I knew my Bible, but I'd never had an honest conversation about what was written with other adult men, and it felt refreshing to have an intentional discussion. I soon learned that the guys were just regular guys, too, dropping various aspects of their lives into the conversation and openly discussing struggles with family and friends. The guy who stood out the most to me was Frank. Frank came into the meeting a few minutes late, and I was startled at first because he closely resembled the husband of one of Emma's friends, a guy who'd been caught cheating on his wife and hidden lots of money from her in his business. But Frank wasn't him. That much was clear after he sat down and shared a brief check-in, speaking about a challenging situation he was having with his teenage daughter and how he was praying God would "soften her heart."

I couldn't believe what I was hearing. Were these guys serious? I had known guys who were family men, who seemed to love their kids and wives, but they'd never shared anything remotely like this stuff. The rest of the evening continued like that, with most of the guys chiming in on the Bible study and sharing whatever else was on their hearts. After a while, they started to close. It was then that a couple of things happened that changed me forever. Both seemed innocuous enough at first, but as they unfolded, I recognized they were much more special. When the group closed for the evening, they ended with a prayer circle, with guys jumping in and offering prayers for other guys, especially if they had a specific request to pray about. Being the new guy, I just sat back and listened. After several guys shared, there was one guy named Matt who absolutely shocked me to my core when he opened his mouth and uttered, "Lord, I lift up John in prayer." Me? One of these guys actually prayed for me, the new guy, a guy who literally just stepped into the room and the group only two hours ago?

Regardless of how much it took me by surprise, it struck me also what that meant coming from him but also for me. A total stranger prayed for me, doing what none of the guys at our old church, nor any of the other guys I knew, had ever offered. It was truly a welcome surprise, but that wasn't the only surprise that I experienced while I was still sitting with everyone. Right after the closing prayer, one of the guys in the group held up his phone, showing on his weather app that a very large thunderstorm was moving into the area at that exact moment. Normally, that would not be a surprise to anyone; however, in the summer of 2012, we were experiencing one of the worst droughts in recent history, to the point that local newspapers were showing pictures of completely empty grain silos. After around six weeks of no rain, it seemed virtually impossible for rain, let alone an actual thunderstorm, to roll through. I got up and said a few goodbyes to some of the guys before heading out to the parking lot, and it was clear through the glass doors that led outside that not only was it raining, it was pouring. I hurriedly made my way to the car, jumped in, and started off on my short drive home, getting to my development and turning onto the main street. As I slowly made my way down the street, I finally saw a few teenage guys on the side of the road with their shirts off, dancing in the rain. While I assumed that was all it was, I did notice that as I drove by, they raised their arms, and it almost looked as though they were cheering, cheering for me as I rolled down the street. I thought that was strange but paid it no mind in the moment. As I reflected on it in the days and weeks after, I thought that maybe there was something else to it, almost a congratulations of sorts.

I walked into the house from the garage, still a little soaked, and made my way upstairs, where Emma was still awake in our bedroom. She asked me the expected questions about how it had worked out. I was definitely in a great mood, but there was something else—it wasn't something I could easily describe, a feeling of ease and relief, as if I had come to the end of a long journey. "You're different," Emma remarked, stating what was becoming increasingly obvious to me. "I know," I replied, then added, "I think I'm going to stick with it and keep showing up." If I just kept going, it might be a great support to me and to our family, but I also knew there was something else going on inside of me, and the feelings I'd experienced that evening were not to be ignored. I spent a lot of time that night and the next morning praying and reflecting on what had happened, and the reality was very clear for me: I truly felt that the presence of God, through Jesus, had come into my heart and brought me a peace I had not had. In my solitude, I asked Jesus to be my Lord and Savior, and I began to hear the inaudible voice of the Spirit speak to me and tell me that this time, it truly was going to be okay.

These early days of becoming a Christian were exciting, as I was relearning the faith of my childhood through a new lens and a new relationship with God. However, there was still a lot of work that had to be done in my life and in that of my family. My marriage was still up in the air, and our future as a family, including where we would live to get Chris the best education, was all but uncertain, yet all I could keep hearing from the Spirit was to just stay the course: "Do not worry about your marriage. Focus on me, learn my Word, and stay with those men." So that was what I did. I continued to attend the men's group and tried to support Emma and Chris in the best ways I could, and slowly, things began to shift, both in our marriage and in our home. While we were still doing counseling, these new circumstances played out in our discussions, and Emma backed off on the July 1 deadline, seeing that I was working and also working on myself. We even tried going to the church that her friend attended and where the men's group met, a stark dichotomy from our experience with the Unitarian church. Where the other church's Sunday school wasn't sure if it could support Chris, the leader at the new one said it was no problem and that we should go enjoy the service. The new church was also a much different experience in terms of the service, something I had never witnessed nor been a part of. Here, the whole congregation was standing, hands in the air, singing at the top of their lungs to the music. The teaching had real value to it and wasn't overly structured or ritualistic like my days in Catholicism—just a pastor standing on the stage in jeans, holding his Bible and speaking from the heart. When Emma and I reflected on these different experiences, it was pretty clear the direction we were going, and in the parking lot outside of our counselor's office one evening, she said she was all in, and we began our lives as believers in Jesus.

The next big hurdle was trying to figure out our living situation. We had to somehow get Chris into a better school district and sell our house, as we were behind on our mortgage and would be forced to do a short sale to get out of it. While our initial conversations revolved around moving into anything, even a one-bedroom apartment, God had other plans and worked a miracle in our favor. Emma's mom, who had been very involved in our lives up until now, offered to buy us a home in the town we identified as having the best school system for Chris. It was not something we ever could have afforded on our own. She had the resources to purchase a three-bedroom, ranch-style home in a well-sought-after part of town, near the retail center and with plenty of access to parks and nature. The purchase was made in the early fall, although there were some updates she agreed to take care of before we moved in, which meant we still had to stay in our old house for a time. While the house was being prepped, we packed up the old house and even had a bunch of the guys from the men's group come and help clean out stuff and move furniture. Once the new house was ready, Emma and Chris were able to move in full-time, but since our home was still on the market and because of the nature of the sale, it still had to be occupied to some degree. So I stayed in the home a few nights a week, then went to the new home the other nights, living with a few pieces of furniture and just enough groceries in the fridge. Finally, on December 31 of that year, the house sale closed, and I pulled out of the garage for the last time that night, feeling both sadness for the trauma we'd experienced there and liberated as I moved into a new life.

The beginning of 2013 saw us slowly move into our next season. Chris had gotten settled in a special education preschool program the district offered, I was working steadily again, and our marriage was greatly repaired thanks to God, continued counseling, and a new church near our home that was very supportive of our family. There were a couple of very profound experiences that we had that year as well, one for me and one for us as a family, that would prove to be significant for years to come. The first took place early in the year. It was a men's ministry event at the church that our counselor attended, and she informed me of it at one of our sessions, saying she'd thought specifically of me when she'd seen it. The event was built around a visit from a guy named Steve Farrar, a pastor who'd written a book called *Point Man* years ago, a sort of "how-to" book for Christian men on marriage and family.

Being very new in my faith, he was not someone I would have ever heard of, but it sounded interesting, so I signed up. The event was held on a Friday night and the following Saturday morning, and it would be a bit of a stretch for me since I was not going with anyone and wouldn't know anyone there, but I felt called to attend and figured I would be just fine solo. The church was a whole other level of experience for me, as it was located in one of the wealthiest suburbs of Chicago. While we lived in an essentially upper-middle-class area, this was way beyond that. The building still maintained the original worship space from the late nineteenth century but had a bunch of modern additions that made it feel more like a museum than a church. I made my way in, got checked in at the registration table, and found a seat toward the front, where I usually preferred to sit during regular church services.

The leader of the men's group came out to introduce Steve, and I was instantly captivated by the guy—very tall and cowboy-ish looking, complete with boots and a big belt buckle (although no hat) and the demeanor and presence of a Texas high school football coach. He started off somewhat even toned in his speaking but gradually got more and more charismatic in his speech, coming right at us as a group of men who needed to be challenged. Whether it was confronting us for only being there because "our wives wanted us to go" or admonishing us for looking at women with lust in our eyes, the guy pulled no punches, and it kept us on the edge of our collective seat. He was also, however, a great teacher of scripture, and the depth of his knowledge became immediately apparent from the beginning of his talk. He started with an examination of the Sermon on the Mount. Specifically, he focused on the section of

Matthew 6, where Jesus speaks on anxiety and worry about one's life, a teaching that I knew very well from my years as a Catholic but also through my new studies with the men's Bible study. Steve stood there and began to rapid-fire through Jesus's words: "Consider the birds of the air, the flowers of the field . . . if God takes care of them, how much more will He care for you." He continued glossing over all the various statements of Jesus, until he abruptly stopped, stared right at the crowd, and challenged us again: "Now, guys, what is Jesus really trying to say here? I'll tell you what he's saying. Two words: Don't panic." I sat in stunned silence and almost immediately slumped back in my seat, part astounded and shocked, part overwhelmed with what I just heard. The words of my father, the words that he'd repeated to me as his mantra over and over again, the words that I'd gotten so sick and tired of hearing all the time—those were the words that he chose to explain one of Jesus's most significant messages.

I drove home that night and began to generate some tears as I thought about what had just happened, as the words of my father now struck me in a way that I'd never expected nor anticipated, words that now had a whole new level of depth and meaning. I was thrown back into my childhood and right back to that dining room table, the one where my father had sat for years, stirring his mixed drink and espousing his famous tag line of "Don't Panic" over and over. I reflected on all the years that I'd heard those words, how much I'd hated my father for giving me words that I'd felt had no meaning—essentially just the ravings of a functional alcoholic. I finally realized that my father had given me perhaps the most profound truth in life, one that may have been too difficult for him to communicate in deep spiritual terms but still carried an essential meaning.

The next day, I returned for the Saturday session and stayed until the very end, after all the other guys who'd wanted to meet Steve had had a chance to stop him and chat. I wound up as the last guy to speak to him. I could tell he was exhausted and anxious to move on to lunch, so I quickly shared exactly what had happened to me the night before, seeing his eyes grow wide with a look of complete astonishment. "Wow, that's a great story. Do you mind if I use it?" I was flattered that he would offer that, and of course, I told him he could. I have wondered all these years how many times he may have actually shared that. I ended the conversation by sharing how much I wanted to step into the man my wife and son really deserved, and he affirmed me with a genuine "Of course you can." I left with a fresh wind under my wings.

The other experience that left a forever impression on me that year would transpire a few months later, this time at a retreat site called Maranatha in central Michigan. When I'd worked as the personal care assistant for the boy with cerebral palsy, the family had shared with me that they'd attended a camp during the summer for families of special needs. The camp, or, more specifically, the retreat, was hosted by an organization called Joni and Friends, founded by a woman named Joni Eareckson Tada, who'd suffered a diving accident as a young woman and had become a quadriplegic. At that time, I had never heard of Joni and Friends nor anything about the retreats for families like ours, but it sure sounded great, so I took it back to Emma, and we started to check it out immediately. Having a child with a disability, we were drawn into it because of how unique and special of an opportunity and environment it was, but it had more meaning for us after we became Christians since it was a faith-based retreat. I remember us spending random days on the laptop, exploring the retreat center online and dreaming of the summer, especially on those cold, snowy days the January before, when we were just stuck in the house. We signed up for the second week they offered, which was the third week in June, allowing our son and his two teacher parents time to finish up their respective school years. Over the months leading up to it, we reviewed the retreat website, looked at all the paperwork we had been sent, and got ourselves packed with everything we needed. The mom of the family I'd served even talked to Emma about the week and everything we would experience. That June, we drove for the very first time to a place that would turn out to have more meaning for me, and my son, than we could have ever imagined.

We drove the almost four hours from the north suburbs of Chicago to the retreat site, Maranatha, outside of Muskegon, Michigan, and made it there on Monday afternoon. We pulled up to the main lodge building and were greeted by a crowd of very energetic and elaborately costumed volunteers, as well as the retreat director. Chris was more than excited to see all the smiling faces. We got out of the car, handed the keys off to the volunteers to park and unload it, and stepped into the lodge building, experiencing something I never expected or imagined. The entire lobby of the building was decorated, partially with sports-related paraphernalia to match the theme for the week. But what stood out more were the welcome signs, the volunteers all dressed up, and most of all, the greeting we received, which, when asked, we requested the "loud version" of. The retreat director grabbed the microphone and spoke into it. "All right, let's give a big Joni and Friends welcome to the Felageller family!" I was literally shaking as the room erupted in thunderous applause for us, mostly for my son Chris. As we walked through the crowd of people, they all cheered for us, and I found it hard to maintain a smile while holding back tears. We made it through to the end of the line and were then greeted by Chris's volunteer buddy for the week, or STM (short-term missionary), named Jane, a kind, middle-aged woman. She directed us to our room in the residential building directly behind the main lodge building, where our luggage had already been deposited by the volunteers who'd taken our car.

After getting settled in, we hurried to dinner back in the main building, then to the Tabernacle, where there was a welcome presentation complete with worship music and some short videos, including some of the ministry founder Joni herself. Once that finished, we went to the social activity for the night that was held outside on the large, open lawn between the main buildings, although that was short-lived since Chris, never one to sit still in those days, showed he was ready to explore. From there, we traveled about a half a mile through a residential area on the property that led straight down to the beach, right on the shores of Lake Michigan, a beach I would come to know well.

Chris could never say no to water or a beach, and while I had lived my whole life in Chicago and spent many a summer day visiting Lake Michigan on some level, I'd never truly seen a beach quite like this. While it was not surrounded by skyscrapers or huge paved sidewalks or bike lanes, it was beautiful in its simplicity, a small beach with sand dunes on one side, and on the other, a playground and a heated pool on a raised deck with wooden swings dangling underneath it. Chris took right to the sand, and we helped him take his shoes off so he could get down and play in it. We decided to take a picture together, with Chris and Emma sitting together on the sand and me hugging them from the top, smiles pasted all over each of us.

We were essentially a family restored. For the first time in months, probably years, we all took a collective breath, partially because of the love we felt from everyone at the retreat site, but also because of the work God had most obviously done in our collective lives. We returned to that beach every day that week—sometimes in the evening, watching the sun go down over the expansive horizon; sometimes in the middle of the day, with Chris playing in the sand or at the playground or in the heated pool above. One morning, while Chris was at the organized program part of the day with his volunteer, Emma and I decided to take a walk to the beach and sit on one of the swings at the encouragement of one of the veteran moms. Sitting on the bench in the mid-morning together, all by ourselves, we looked out at the waves crashing onto the sand, reflecting on God's blessings and how he had carried us all this way and how grateful we were to have found Him. "See, honey?" I said to Emma. "We made it this far. We made it to the beach at Maranatha, and if we can make it here, then maybe we can make it a little bit farther."

Every saint has a past,
and every sinner has a future.

—OSCAR WILDE—

6 the divorce

"PUT YOUR COAT ON. We need to go into the garage and have a talk."

Huh? What was this about? Emma had walked right up to me after stepping back into the house, patted me on the chest a couple of times, and, with a wry smile and chipper demeanor, invited me to step outside and have a very unexpected talk. It was Black Friday, the day after Thanksgiving 2019, and I'd been having a very plain, simple day up until that point, avoiding the crazy retail madness as usual and choosing instead to putter around the house while Chris was visiting a family friend and Emma was out, presumably running errands. It had been a relatively quiet holiday that year, with me running down to visit my mom briefly and have lunch with her since she no longer did big Thanksgiving meals as she had gotten older and struggled with mobility issues, and with Emma deciding to stay back home. That was not unusual—Chris always had challenges being in an environment that wasn't more childproofed, or "Chris-proofed," as we called it, and it was always hard to watch him and enjoy a meal. Plus, we'd had friends over to the house like normal this year, although our gathering had been much smaller than in the past, essentially just my close friend's family. So it had been a very uneventful, though not odd, holiday, at least until now. With a fair amount of confusion and perplexity, I grabbed a coat and headed out to the garage.

To my surprise, there were two camping chairs sitting in the middle of it, with the garage door still wide open. I sat in one chair, and Emma sat right next to me, proceeding to take out a letter and read it to me. It started with a very ominous, "John, I love you, but I can't be married to you anymore. I am divorcing you and am hoping that we can work together as co-parents." My heart sank in my chest, and I slumped into the chair, the weight of the sun, moon, and stars collectively feeling like they had just been thrown on my shoulders. She handed me the letter and stood up, saying she was going to get Chris and take him with her for a few days to give me space to process and time to move out of our bedroom and into the guest room. As she hurriedly moved back into the house to grab a few things before she left, I desperately tried to interject with whatever I could get out of my mouth.

"Why are you doing this? What did I do? Can we work on this?" She clearly had a plan and tried to avoid my questions, continuing to move quickly in and out of the house, giving flippant responses that essentially put the blame on fights we'd had a few years ago.

How could those affect any decision like this right now? We had put so much time into working on our marriage, spending years in counseling—successfully, so I thought—to the point that we hadn't gone for regular sessions for some time, except if we had a random fight. The last big fight we'd had was almost two years ago, and we had worked it out almost immediately, even going back to the counselor to make sure we'd worked it out, so how did we get here?

Emma took her things, including the family dog, and headed out the door—no tears, no emotions, just focused on her task at hand. Now completed, she walked out of the house and out of my life as I watched in shock. I went back into the house and stood in the kitchen with my head spinning, holding the sink to keep myself upright. I had no clue what to do next or how to proceed, although I knew I couldn't stay in the house because I would drive myself crazy. So I did the only thing I could think of: I jumped in the car and went for a drive, ending up in the parking lot of a local retail area. I realized that I would need to talk to someone for advice or just to vent. I contemplated my situation just like I had all those years ago, sitting in the parking lot of the church and feeling utterly desperate. This time, however, was very different from what I had experienced seven years ago. As I thought about who I needed to call and who could help me, I started to riffle through the Rolodex in my head of all my contacts. Unlike the last time I'd sat in that car and felt hopeless, this time, I discovered that I had much more support than before, mostly due to the fact that I'd realized back then everything I hadn't had and become very intentional about building and finding community. When I had started my journey as a Christian and learned from good, strong men how to build myself back up, I had also tried to find support as a special needs parent and, specifically, a special needs father. In some ways, I wondered if all the work I had done and was still doing in the special needs and disability world—advocacy work and writing and speaking and being part of a variety of parent support groups, including those for dads—had affected Emma's feelings about me and us somehow.

This work was a more recent development in my life, but once it had begun, it moved quickly, and I found myself doing a whole variety of things with several different organizations and ministries around the country. I developed relationships with many significant people in that world. It actually began quite simply: After several years of working on our marriage and rebuilding myself as a man through our church, I started to feel the desire to do more and give back.

Initially, this started with getting involved with other special needs dads in my area. This included joining a couple of Facebook groups and, eventually, starting a meetup for special needs dads in my own neighborhood. We also attracted dads from other nearby towns. But my real passion was, and always had been, writing, so as I pursued my goal of wanting to be a writer, I reached out to some of the special needs parents I had met through the Joni and Friends family retreat. I knew several of them were authors, and I eventually connected with one mom from the Chicago area who had published a book and was also a blogger with a disability ministry in the Midwest. Although I had only ever been interested in writing a book, she suggested blogging. The ministry she worked with was always looking for more writers, and they especially wanted to have more dad writers. Plus, blogging would give me some experience and exposure. At first, I hesitated since it wasn't what I really wanted to do, but I gave it a try and found that it was actually quite enjoyable. I even received some positive feedback from my fellow writers.

About six months later, at the end of 2017, I received word that the small local ministry I was writing for was merging with Key Ministry, a larger, more national disability ministry that had a huge following on social media. Realizing how big they were, I was quite intimidated. But I couldn't say no to the opportunity, so I agreed to come on board with them as a writer and joined a group of national authors, speakers, and experts in the disability ministry world. That was really the beginning of my journey into advocacy.

In the spring of 2018, I received my first invitation to speak at Inclusion Fusion Live, Key Ministry's yearly conference held at their home church of Bay Presbyterian Church in Bay Village, Ohio, just outside of Cleveland. I was invited to speak on a dads panel from the main stage with two guys I had never met before: Jason Hague, who was an author, and Jonathan McGuire, who ran a disability ministry with his wife, Sarah. I remember meeting them briefly before we went on stage, and we seemed to have a decent rapport, which helped the small amount of butterflies I had in my stomach, having not done anything like this before. Our panel seemed to be well-received by everyone who heard it, and I enjoyed spending the rest of the conference meeting getting to know a variety of disability leaders from around the country. These included people who were or would eventually become "household names" in disability ministry, including Steve Grcevich, the Key Ministry founder, and others like Jolene Philo, Emily Colson, and Sandra Peoples. These friendships eventually led me to continue to blog for Key Ministry, as well as a couple of other ministries, including Hope Anew. I was even published on *The Mighty*, a well-known disability support and resources website that was secular and very respected. I also received more opportunities to speak at other disability-related conferences, like Wonderfully Made in Kansas City, and was interviewed on disability-related podcasts, the first one being *A Special Hope*, which my friend Sarah Broady created. In the next year, I befriended many other local disability advocates and connected with newer national organizations like the Special Fathers Network, founded by David Hirsch, a Chicago executive. Through him, I made a lot of connections with some prominent names among men and dads who were involved with disability advocacy, including some local celebrities, and even helped start the first-ever annual conference for the Special Fathers Network. Over the years, I'd dedicated much of my time to making the world a better place for people with disabilities, especially Chris, and didn't see myself stopping.

Now, sitting in my car once again, I asked myself a simple question: "Who can I call?" I could answer that much more easily and quickly because of everything I had experienced, so I leaned into what I had. The first person I reached out to was a guy named Jeff, a special needs attorney who also had a child with a disability and was also divorced. I initially messaged him on Facebook and was somewhat surprised when he asked me to call him back at his office. He turned out to be exactly the right guy I needed to hear from. We talked for about fifteen minutes, and he was blunt but caring, explaining that this was not something that Emma had just planned yesterday—it was something she had been planning for some time. He passed along the name of his divorce attorney, who was exactly the person I wound up using, and I continued to reach out to other dads and ministry friends. Some of the guys from my various dad groups were divorced and gave me both advice and support. One person I reached out to was one of my best friends Sam, who had just been at my home the previous night for Thanksgiving, and upon receiving the text from me about what had happened, he thought I was joking, not being able to believe what he was hearing.

We agreed to meet the next afternoon after he finished some family appointments. I was meeting with another friend in the morning, but I found that I had some time to kill before I met him, so I decided to go to the local Catholic church. The church had hours for confession at that time on Saturdays, and I thought there would be no harm in speaking to a priest for support given my circumstances. I had not been to confession in years, but it was, for anyone raised Catholic, something that was natural after being raised in the faith for so long, and now, even as an evangelical, I still respected it for the element of spiritual intercession. I walked into the booth, closed the door behind me, and kneeled facing the two-way window. I started in the usual fashion: "Bless me, Father, for I have sinned . . ." and proceeded to share what had just occurred. The priest listened to my side, and while I freely admitted to any sin I had committed in the marriage—mainly hurting Emma's feelings and arguing with her—he was empathetic to my side and simply said, "Those sound like the actions of a fourteen-year-old."

I might have managed a smile if I hadn't been in so much pain. The priest followed up with some instructions for me. "I want you to say the Lord's Prayer every day for a week, and say it very slowly and intentionally." Sounded easy enough, but then he followed up with a question: "When you hear the first words of that prayer, the Our Father, what do those words mean to you?"

"Hmm," I pondered. "That I have a Father in heaven who cares for me? That he loves me and won't abandon me? That if he is my Father, then I am his child, and he won't abandon me?"

"Yes," he replied, "but it also means you have brothers and sisters in Christ who will stand by you and walk with you and support you while you are going through this ordeal."

As I moved forward with that advice and with the support of a whole slew of friends and ministry supporters, I faced the reality of going ahead with the divorce process. First, we connected with our marriage counselor, whom Emma had suggested be on our divorce team to help us negotiate parenting. But there was another layer to her involvement: Emma had been seeing her for several weeks prior to leaving me, and while I'd been aware she'd been seeing her and struggling with some things, I had not known that the conversation had come to this. I had not initially been concerned about

Emma going to see her, especially since we would speak to her about things on a random basis, and I'd been very upfront about asking if she'd wanted me involved. She'd said no. So in order to feel comfortable agreeing to her being on the divorce team, I went first to meet with the counselor alone, who explained that it had not been her intention to keep me out of the loop, but Emma had refused to bring me into the discussion once it'd gotten that far. A couple of days after that meeting, the two of us met with the counselor to consider her role on the team, but my goal was to hopefully get some answers. I had been counseled by many personal and ministry friends, some of whom had pastoral and counseling backgrounds, to not react with anger or frustration to anything said but instead to ask questions and listen. As I sat and asked some basic questions about why she'd made the decision, she proceeded with a laundry list of grievances, almost all of them from years ago, items that I thought we were over. But then she said something that was both extremely telling and just as hurtful: "All that blogging and speaking stuff you do, I don't want anything to do with that." That was a huge revelation, and everything started to make a little more sense to me. Did Emma really feel as though the advocacy and ministry work I was doing was pulling me away from the family?

I reflected in the moment about how loaded that comment was. Sitting with a fair amount of shock, I was instantly pulled back into a bunch of memories over the last couple of years, many of which involved Emma showing and speaking about how proud she was of me for what I was doing in ministry. Yet I also quickly realized that underneath, there was a lot of resentment toward me for what Emma had perceived as my wanting to focus more on the ministry work than her or Chris. There was a comment made about the time I had gone to a ministry conference in Kansas City, and she'd gotten the flu after I had already left. Once she'd informed me of that, I'd made sure to come home as it was over, dropping my bags and taking over the situation. I also considered the events of the past spring, when Chris had developed a seizure disorder out of nowhere one weekend. Upon taking him to the hospital, we'd discovered that he had a condition called a Chiari malformation. This was a malformation of the skull that put pressure on the brain and resulted, in Chris's case at least, in repeated grand mal seizures over a couple of days. We'd spent several days in the hospital, and once he had stabilized, we'd made plans to have the corrective surgery the next month, which involved removing a small part of his skull and the top T1 vertebrae. The day we'd brought him to the hospital for the procedure had been one of the hardest of my life. I can still feel his body shaking from fear when we'd first arrived—I'd just held him tightly and whispered to him that he was going to be okay, not really sure if he would be. After a few hours of prep and time in surgery, he'd come out of the procedure successfully, and we'd gone home to support Chris's recovery, which had meant about six weeks of relative bed rest. Emma had taken family medical leave from her teaching job to be home.

Was she feeling unresolved anger for what she perceived as having to take more care of Chris in that moment, even though that was what we'd agreed to and I'd been as present as I could be while still going to work?

The rest of the session was extremely uncomfortable, with Emma continuing to espouse a variety of points of anger she had toward me and the marriage. Still being in a fair amount of emotional vulnerability, I sat there and listened, hoping to hear an answer, but none came. The counselor was able to calm Emma down and get us to both agree to move forward with the divorce process, but she explained she could no longer work with us personally, which we agreed to. The dynamic between Emma and me the next few months was civil but certainly not peaceful. I felt like a stranger in my own home, having moved into the guest bedroom, while still honoring my responsibilities to Chris. We were able to make it through the remainder of the holidays, although it was now very strange helping Chris buy presents for his mom since I no longer felt the same love or connection while picking out cards or presents for her. In January of 2020, we started meeting with the divorce team, and as we had agreed to a collaborative divorce, both sides met and discussed the points of the divorce together.

From start to finish, it took a little over three months. While certainly not without disagreements or struggles in the negotiation, for the most part, we were civil and respectful to each other, always reminded by the professionals to keep Chris at the center. Things smoothed out between us over those few months, helped along when I moved out in March and got my own apartment about twenty minutes north of the house we'd previously shared together. It was also an odd help that the COVID-19 pandemic hit shortly after I'd moved out. Due to the severe restrictions in society, I felt it even more necessary to work together to support each other. The legitimate fear I felt for what was happening in our country and world brought me to a level of empathy that I don't think I would have reached without it.

In April of 2020, a couple of weeks after my birthday, I was formally divorced from Emma after fifteen years of marriage, and in the most surreal way—it happened over a conference call, as courts were not open, but I was grateful I didn't have to see her in person. That morning, I struggled mightily. Regardless of how much peace I thought I had achieved up until that point, the truth was that I was an emotional wreck. I listened to the Sinead O'Connor song "The Last Day of Our Acquaintance" on repeat, a song lamenting a failed marriage that described the final moments of a divorce. I received many messages and texts from all the friends and ministry folk who had supported me, but there was one that especially stuck out to me—the one from my friend Wayne Messmer. Wayne was no ordinary guy, as he was, for all intents and purposes, a local celebrity, a guy I had met through my friend David Hirsch in our shared work with the Special Fathers Network. Wayne was known in Chicago as "the Voice," an icon who was best known for singing the national anthem at a variety of sporting events, some of the more notable ones being at the 1991 NHL All-Star Game at the legendary Chicago Stadium and at the 2016 World Series at the equally legendary Wrigley Field. He was also an accomplished singer outside of that, recording his own albums of American standards and classics and performing with his own quartets or big bands around the city. He had a whole bunch of other accolades to his credit—star of live theatre, radio host, and one of the founders of the Chicago Wolves hockey team. I had slowly developed a relationship with Wayne over several months in 2019, eventually meeting for breakfast one morning to discuss ways to work together on some projects, but a real friendship had developed soon after.

It had been about a month after that first breakfast that he'd invited me out to see him in a performance of his one-man stage show based on the life of Father Damien, a Dutch Catholic priest who had achieved sainthood for his work with the leper colony in Moloka'i, Hawaii, back in the late 1800s. Wayne performed the shows in a variety of different venues, but it worked especially well when he performed in a Catholic church, and that was where

I'd seen him perform it for the first time. I'd arrived at a smaller community church in the northwest suburbs of Chicago that night in November 2019, and after greeting Wayne and his wife in the foyer, I'd taken my seat in a pew toward the front of the sanctuary, sitting among folks probably thirty years my senior. Wayne had come out and taken his place on the altar, which had essentially acted as the stage that night. There'd been some simple props to accentuate the tropical location and a screen that had still pictures projected onto it. Wearing full priestly regalia, he'd begun the show, unfolding the life and experiences of Damien, from his youth to his days serving the lepers in Moloka'i. After almost ninety minutes of his performance, he'd closed the show by turning to the crucifix hanging above the altar and uttering these iconic final words: "In all that I have done, for good or for ill, I am your priest, and you are my God, and I trust in your prodigious love." I'd walked out of the church that night affected greatly by the words I'd heard, feeling as though they would mean something profound for me in the near future, and they actually did, one week later. It was the very next Friday, Black Friday of 2019, that I received divorce papers from Emma, and it was then that I knew I'd been in that seat at the show for a reason, almost as if God had known it was a message I would need for what was coming. Those words carried me through my divorce, and for the next months and years following it, they were a strong reminder that regardless of how things had turned out, I was never alone or abandoned by God.

The months and years ahead saw me settle into a new dynamic—that of a single, divorced dad who only saw his son on select days or weekends. I cared for him the best I could when I had him, but I dealt with extreme loneliness when he wasn't around. I certainly had lots of support from friends, and I was blessed that so many had shown up for me when I'd needed them, but people couldn't be available every second of the day, and COVID-19 didn't help matters. On nights without my son, I went to sleep pining for the days when I could be under one roof with my family. Being single, with my father having passed away years ago, my mother being in assisted living with dementia, and having no siblings, made it very difficult for me. But the days with Chris were more precious than ever, and I poured all my love into him, trying my best to make all the moments with him special. Like the days when he'd been very young and we'd spent most week-ends together, the focus was solely on my relationship with him. I loved going on long walks with him in the woods near my apartment or taking short trips with him during the summer. The hard days with him were made even harder by the fact that I didn't have a partner to share the responsibilities with, someone I could "tag in" when I needed help cleaning up vomit or bathroom ac-cidents, keeping him occupied while I tried to finish my meal, or helping him eat.

Once, we were walking in one of his favorite forest preserves, Independence Grove, located in the far north suburbs of Chicago. It was a very picturesque place that he had spent many days at as a young boy when we'd lived very close to there. Now, we visited occasionally on weekends. We walked the paved paths along open green spaces and the large man-made lake in the middle, and I talked to him about days past when we'd walked there years ago and he'd been much smaller and had much more energy. "It's kinda lonely walking all by ourselves, huh, buddy? Maybe someone special will join us sometime and we can be a whole family again. Maybe God will do that."

The glory of Christianity is to conquer by forgiveness.

—WILLIAM BLAKE—

7 the redemption

"YOU DON'T KNOW ME, but I know who you are."

Hmm. That was interesting. Who was this person? I had pulled over to stop for gas a few minutes from the house I was renting in the far north suburbs after coming from a meeting with a church networking group in Chicago. It was December of 2023, and after many years of teaching in one form or another, I was finally working full-time in disability ministry. I'd accepted a job working for Joni and Friends in their Chicago office. I'd landed the job in the spring of 2022 when the Montessori school I'd been working at near downtown was closing because of low enrollment. I'd discovered the opening when I was in a virtual meeting for local ministries. I'd been hired as a ministry relations manager, which meant I essentially worked with churches to help them build and develop disability ministries. I'd been struggling to meet someone, mainly because finding someone who shared my spiritual beliefs and who could fit into Chris's life was a stretch. But on that day, in my car at the gas station, I opened up the Christian dating app I had been on for a few months and discovered this new woman who'd matched with me—someone I didn't recognize but who apparently knew me.

I glanced over the profile of this lovely woman named Faith, whose picture was quite striking to me, and as I looked at her other pictures and bio, I tried to get a clue about how she knew me. Finally, I read her response to a prompt about what a great activity to do together would be: "Let's volunteer at a Joni and Friends family retreat." What? She must be associated with the ministry, but I had no idea how, although I assumed from her answer that she was a volunteer at our family retreats—the same ones that I had brought Chris to for years and that I now worked at every summer. I responded curiously, asking how she knew me and how she was involved with us, and she replied that she had been at the retreat this last summer and had seen me with my son. That would have been the second week in June, when I'd decided to try to bring Chris as a single dad for the first time while also being a staff member. It had been an especially challenging week—the weather had been extremely cold for that time of the year, so we had been unable to be outside much, which was one of Chris's favorite things to do, and because of the lower temperatures, he'd developed a mild cold. That, of course, had meant that since Chris could not blow his nose, he had to release all the backed-up congestion by throwing up, which was exactly what he'd done two nights in a row. Being alone, I'd had to clean it all up myself. Dealing with that, managing Chris's service dog, and completing all my other responsibilities had just been too overwhelming for me to notice anyone noticing me.

What I did not realize was that she had a long relationship with Joni and Friends. She'd been a family retreat volunteer for many years, both at the Michigan retreats and at some of the other locations, and belonged to a church that had a long history of sending families and volunteers to attend. What I also didn't know was that while the two of us were messaging each other, Faith reached out to my boss, our area director, Michelle, who was actually an old friend of hers. While she grilled Michelle for all the details on me, she reacted to my quick responses to her on the app: "You got back to me pretty quick, it seems."

Admittedly, I had, so what did I say? I sent the first thing that popped into my head: "Well, I felt the prompting of the Holy Spirit to reach out." That sounded good, I thought. It actually went way better than I'd expected, as I wasn't aware that Faith attended a very "charismatic" Christian church, meaning there was a special emphasis on the Holy Spirit.

Upon reading that, she came back with what could only be described as astonishment: "Did Michelle tell you to say that?" *No, why would you ask me that?* I pondered. Because she had just asked Michelle the question, "Does he know the Holy Spirit?" which she would share with me later on. This was getting interesting, and considering how quick and easy the conversation was going, I decided to go for it: "Are you free to grab some coffee tonight?" She said she had to teach a kids church class that evening, but maybe we could meet tomorrow, so I agreed to dinner near our ministry office.

My experience dating the last few years since the divorce had not been very enjoyable. Although I'd certainly tried to meet someone and had definitely had my share of first dates, there had never been really a match for a variety of reasons. I had dated a couple of women for a few months, but neither relationship had gone anywhere, even though they'd both identified as Christian and had seemed accepting of Chris at least. Being someone who attended church regularly, volunteered at church, engaged in lots of advocacy work, and was a single father to a child with a disability definitely limited my choices with women. Still, I went on my first date with Faith with a fair amount of optimism based on what I knew and what I hoped for from our brief interactions. The restaurant I chose was a familiar place, somewhere close to my office where we had eaten for work celebrations a few times. It was casual but also nice enough to qualify for a first date, and I headed straight there after I finished for the day. I arrived at the restaurant a little early and got a table, and with the few minutes I thought I had before she came, I decided to run to the bathroom quickly. While I was in the bathroom, Faith came into the restaurant and did a quick scan looking for me in the general direction of where I'd texted her that I was sitting. Upon not seeing me, she later confessed that her first instinct was that she had been stood up, but because she had waited so long to actually sit down and meet me, she decided to wait, and when I spotted her by the door, I walked up and escorted her to the table.

Our first date seemed to be a culmination of everything all the other first dates hadn't been. We instantly clicked, and there was a strong level of comfort from the beginning but also an old-fashioned innocence. It didn't take long for us to start putting our cards on the table in terms of what we were looking for.

"So Chris has a pretty severe disability and requires a lot of hands-on care."

Her face crinkled in a look that said, *Are you serious?* "You know I'm a nurse, right, and I've been volunteering at Joni and Friends for years?" I was glad to hear that response and quite relieved that it wasn't going to be a problem, as that always had the potential to be a dealbreaker, but then she put her own dealbreaker out there: "I don't want to date anyone forever. I'm not looking for a friend to go to the movies with . . . I want marriage, not just a relationship. Are you interested in that?"

If that statement was made by anyone else on any other date, I would have probably recoiled, especially on a first date—while I was very interested in being married again, I assumed that even if I met someone, the timeline from a first date to the aisle would be years. But instead of wanting to get up and leave, a sense of calm washed over me. I responded that that was what I was looking for, too, even though she made a comment about how I'd put "seeking a relationship" on my profile. "I just put that because that's what most people are looking for. Of course, I want to be married, but not everyone is ready for that in the beginning." We agreed that we wanted the same thing, and before the date ended, my mouth opened, and the following words spilled out: "I am so gonna marry you." While I normally would have considered that putting my foot in my mouth, it actually felt right.

Leaving the restaurant that night, I had the stark reality that I not only had entered into a new relationship but had also possibly met my new wife, and my life in the short term was probably going to change fairly rapidly. But there was one more huge change that was also floating around, and it had to do with Chris's school placement, as he had been having a very difficult sophomore year. Since the divorce, Chris had seemed to handle the changes pretty well, and while he had displayed some aggression during junior high, which we'd chalked up to the beginnings of adolescence, he had, for the most part, not had any issues. This school year, however, was a very different story. Chris was having regular outbursts of aggression at home with Emma and me, as well as at school with most of his staff and teachers. Initially, we discovered that he had a severe GI blockage, which was probably the catalyst, but even after he got treatment, he was still displaying aggression with everyone. Although the school staff tried to manage his behavior, including the school nurse giving him a mood stabilizer prescribed by his psychiatrist, they were frequently out of options, leaving them to call us to come pick him up. While I had the benefit of being able to work from home a fair amount of time, it was still a challenge for me to stop working at any given moment, and in Emma's case, it was even more challenging with her teaching job. After many discussions and meetings with a variety of his staff and teachers, a decision was made to start looking for an alternative placement, so with the help of the school, Emma and I began exploring options for a new school.

Overall, there was change coming into my life—some wanted, most unexpected, and all a little scary. I went into the holiday season that year probably busier than I had been in a while. After our first date, it didn't take long for Faith to start inviting me into her life in very personal ways, first with a visit to her church, then to meet her mom, all in one weekend.

Coming to church with her was a huge step since it was a small neighborhood church where everyone knew each other and where all the families had belonged to the church for generations. It was also a church that had long-standing ties to Joni and Friends, with many families both serving with the ministry and also attending the retreats if they had a child with a disability, and I was pleasantly surprised to see folks I recognized from years past. The next day, we made plans to meet her mom, who was going to be at a very large mall in our area, and while it was a short meeting, it went about as well as expected given the short notice. On Christmas Eve, we went to a night service at my friend Sam's church with his family, and I was excited to not only spend Christmas Eve together but also to celebrate with Faith and have her meet a close friend.

Despite whatever concerns I had about how things would work out, for both Chris and me, that Christmas was one of the most enjoyable and loving ones I had felt in a long time—I didn't have to worry about being lonely during the holidays anymore.

The beginning of 2024 saw our relationship grow very steadily and quickly, and although we were not officially engaged, we began to talk about the possibility of planning a wedding, quite possibly in the next few months. While our intention was not to rush, we knew that we wanted to be married sooner rather than later, but we also had to consider Chris's situation.

After going through the process of trying to find a new school placement for him that was close to home, he was repeatedly denied by almost all the potential places, except for one. This one, a therapeutic day school with residential living facilities in Wichita, Kansas, reached back out to us and said they would absolutely consider his application. Upon discussing this with Emma and getting many wonderful recommendations from people we spoke with, we agreed this was the best placement and choice for him, so we decided to pursue his education there. Chris was accepted a short time later; however, this also meant that he would be required to enroll at the school in a given timeframe and essentially put us at the beginning of June for Chris leaving. So we prayerfully considered the options, and we agreed that if we were going to get married, we wanted Chris to be there. We started to do some initial planning in terms of where we could get married and what we wanted it to look like and also considered some dates that might work prior to his leaving in June. I worked on getting the best ring I could afford—not easy for a single dad whose budget had become stretched pretty thin over the years—but I was pleased with what I found, and I started to plan a proposal.

The day I proposed, I invited Faith to come over to my place on a Sunday, and while it was late morning, I tried to make it as romantic as I possibly could. To do that, I decided to turn off all the lights, light the numerous LED candles I had, and stream the live feed from a place that was very special to us separately but now had a unique meaning for us as a couple. That place was Maranatha, specifically the beach—the place where I'd been restored years ago, the place where I'd shared so many wonderful memories with Chris. But even more than that, it was a place where both of us had spent many days walking on our own, me after my divorce and her for years before we met, praying that God would bring our true loves to us. It was a place that meant so much to us that our photographer friend Jake, who had taken pictures at the retreats for years, had sent us a picture of the beach at sunset, a picture we wound up using as a backdrop at the wedding. After settling in, I brought her to the carpet right in front of the TV and the live camera feed of the beach, the early spring waves crashing against the shore. While we both knew what the answer would be, the moment was just as sweet and tender, and within moments, we were officially engaged. To celebrate, we walked and took pictures of her wearing the ring at Independence Grove, the place where I walked with Chris so often, the place where I prayed with him to give us the missing piece for our family. A place where we now shared the beginning of our new life together.

Planning the wedding was no small task, as we had a very short timeframe and wanted to have as big a celebration as possible. The first goal, of course, was to find a venue, which was not easy given the short notice we were working with. Initially, we considered the large courtyard at Faith's church; however, 2024 was the year of the "cicada apocalypse," with part of the Midwest facing the almost twenty-year emergence of the largest brood of the big-eyed buggies. So an outdoor wedding was out of the question, and the other church in the community that some families had used for an indoor service wasn't available. Leaning into the church relationships I had because of my job with Joni and Friends, I reached out to my friend Rick, who led a disability ministry at a large church in our area. He connected me with the event planner there, and she met with us and discussed the options. It was clear from the beginning that it was more than just the only choice—it was the best choice. The space the church used for weddings was the exact same space that Rick used for his disability ministry, as they did their own dedicated service on Sunday nights, so it fit who we were perfectly. It was essentially a gym/all-purpose space, with large windows and a stage, practical enough to host a larger wedding but also nice enough for something more formal as well. While we were unsure about the exact date we should choose, I had an experience driving to a church meeting a little while after meeting with the event planner. I was listening to a Moody Radio show in the car in which a couple who were marriage counselors talked about how they got married "five months and five days" after their first date.

So five months and five days after our first date, on May 19, 2024, we got married among family and friends at Rick's church in the space where his "Front Porch Church" all-abilities service was held. I was in awe of the way that everyone from her church pitched in, from the event planning and the decorations to the music during and after the ceremony. I'd found a great caterer through someone at our Joni and Friends office, and our cake had been made by Moose & Me, a local disability-friendly bakery named after the family's daughter with a disability. There were lots of elements of our mutual path serving in disability ministry throughout the day, but there were some other very special aspects to the ceremony related to both family and friends. The most special part for me was Chris's involvement, as my hope was that he would be my best man, at least symbolically, although I knew he wouldn't be able to stand up front very long. To help support him, we had his Special Olympics coach from the local YMCA, Coach Tom, and Katherine, one of his PCAs, to help redirect and keep a steady hand on him. I also had my friend Sam serve as my stand-in best man—although I knew he would essentially be my actual best man—standing with me through the whole ceremony. But Chris, to my amazement, stood with his helpers through all of it, only stepping down from the stage once Faith came out and staying off the side. Having him there with me made the whole experience complete, and I beamed with pride as my severely autistic son did not have to be relegated to a corner of the room or even another room entirely; he was with me the whole time.

The other special memory of the day was our wedding song, which was lavishly performed by my dear friend Wayne, a man whose voice had filled countless stadiums and live music stages, a voice that now lent itself to starting our new life together. I certainly wanted Wayne to sing not only because of his voice but also because of what his friendship had meant to me over the last few years since my divorce. The song we chose was actually an old favorite of mine, "We Have All the Time in the World," a jazzy romantic tune originally sung by the legendary crooner Louis Armstrong. It was also the theme song from one of my all-time favorite movies, *On Her Majesty's Secret Service*, a James Bond film from the 1960s that featured Bond finally falling in love and getting married. Even though the ending of the film was not pleasant, the love story that was the background of the entire film always resonated with me. After the ceremony and dinner started, we cut the cake, then proceeded with our first dance. As I introduced Wayne as our special guest singer, I related the story of how I'd met him, the impact his life had had on mine, and how his example had affected me. The music cued up, and as Wayne belted out the first line, I could feel the power and the emotion in his voice, and I smiled a little inside, thinking about how my words might have affected his singing. I held my new bride close as we danced in the small area to the side of the space, and for five minutes, life was more perfect than I could have imagined just a few months earlier; in that moment, all the frustration I'd experienced over the last few years just melted away. Following the song, we grabbed some pictures together, then invited Chris and his service dog out onto the floor with us as "We Are Family" played in the background, a very sweet and tender moment to add to so many we had that night.

The night of the wedding, we stayed at a hotel near the church, then drove home the next day to enjoy a few days of rest. Although once we arrived, we discovered a front room filled with gifts and packages, and we did our best to corral them so we could move around. After some dinner and a movie, we decided to go ahead and open gifts, so in no particular order, I started grabbing whatever seemed closest to me. Each time I picked up a bag or a wrapped gift, I always searched for the card first, as we meticulously made a list of every gift and who had given it to us. I finally came to the last bag, and for whatever reason, I decided to take the gift out of the bag first instead of the card, and upon placing my hands inside the bag, I pulled out a very nice pewter wedding sculpture of a large heart with a smaller heart inside. Hanging from the smaller heart was a small cross, and there was a tag on the bottom with the sentiment of how to keep Christ in the middle of your marriage, a wonderful sentiment that could have only come from a nice grandmother type from our church. Or so I thought. I reached into the bag and pulled out the card, and upon opening it, I paused, put my head in my hands, and took a deep breath. The card was from Chris, a gift for his father and new stepmom on their wedding day, certainly a very significant thing to receive from your child for this special day, but there was more to the gift and the card than just that. Anytime Emma or I would receive a gift from Chris, we knew that the gift essentially came from each other, as Chris didn't have the cognitive skills to be able to shop for and pick out gifts for his parents. That gift and the card with the lovely sentiment written in coherent handwriting, except for Chris's signature, were from his mom and my ex as much as they were from him.

Sitting with that realization, I came to a full-circle understanding of everything that I had experienced, now reflecting on a lifetime of memories, some filled with love, some filled with rage and anger, some even full of fear. I looked back at the struggles of childhood and adolescence; the hopes and dreams of a first marriage that inevitably failed; the birth of a son who, despite all the challenges I faced raising him, still gifted me more than I could have hoped or imagined. Now, after the pain of divorce, I sat with my new wife, having reached a place of restoration and redemption for myself. Even more so, I came to a full awareness of the power of forgiveness,

forgiveness for Emma and also for my parents, especially my father. A father who, on the surface, gave me nothing, no coaching, no real support, yet also gave me the most important advice of all. A man whom I watched sit and stir his drink at that dining room table my whole life, seeming mostly indifferent to his life and family, still passed on the most valuable inheritance. I now understood what he'd been trying to teach me all those years ago, repeating his exhaustive catchphrase of "Don't Panic" over and over again. In doing the least he could manage to parent me, he actually provided more than I could imagine. I could now appreciate its full meaning. I thought about all the wonderful teachers and mentors I'd had over the years, ones who had led me to Christ but had also spoken into my life, showing me the value of love and forgiveness. The moments of struggle and pain had value, as they taught me what it truly meant to lean into the hope of God when my situation became too overwhelming. I shared all of this with Faith on the couch together that evening, and we embraced in tears with a knowing that we had been led through storms and valleys in both our lives to find each other by a God who would never abandon or forsake us. Afterward, I stood up from the couch, picking up the sculpture and setting it on the TV cabinet to admire from the other side of the room, a true marker of an incredible milestone in my life.

I smiled.

afterword

THE STORY you have just read is absolutely true, as it is, in fact, my life's journey. In the process of working on this project, I have had several friends ask me the logical question, "Who is this being written for?" That can be answered in a variety of ways, as I believe it is a story that appeals to several different kinds of readers. It is certainly written for parents of special needs children, especially dads, whom I have always uniquely identified with and have sought to support through my various outreaches. But it is certainly also a story for moms of special needs children, as I feel they can still very much relate to all the aspects of raising a child with a disability that I've shared here. This is also a story for couples and families who, while they may not identify with disability, can still relate to the different struggles that I experienced in my first marriage. Ultimately, though, it is a story of redemption and forgiveness, of experiencing the love of Jesus Christ in the hardest times and the most unlikely of places. So it is also written for the person who may be hanging on by a thread in their lives, for the person who needs a reminder that despite their circumstances, they are loved by God, and their rescue could be just around the corner.

To each of these groups, I say the following:

For the parents of special needs children . . . your lives will always carry more weight and stress than that of a typical family. You did not ask for these circumstances, but they are yours nonetheless, and the true gift in this journey is loving your child above all else—because they are yours, wonderfully made by our Creator. I encourage you to learn to embrace the journey as I did, to learn to lean into God on the hard days, to remember to support each other through every valley and trial, and to appreciate the blessings that come in even the smallest packages. Most of all, remember that you are seen, you are loved, you are worthy, and you matter to your kids.

To the fathers of special needs children . . . you have a special role in the life of your child, but your journey is different from that of your spouse, the mother of your children. You deal with the same guilt and shame that moms carry, but you process yours in different ways, and frequently, that equates to you carrying those emotions rather than expressing them. You may find yourself throwing yourself into your work, hoping to provide for all the needs that are now on your plate, while also withdrawing from your family and marriage, whether consciously or not. For you, I encourage you to find "that guy," or better yet, a group of guys, with whom you can connect, share your life, and process all the emotions that go along with raising your unique child. Be willing to engage in the various ways you would for any typical child and find creative ways to mimic those experiences in ways that work for your kids. Most of all, don't do this alone, as there are resources and support for you as well. And if you have no one to connect with, as I always say, please reach out to me. I am always available to help a fellow dad out.

For anyone else who may relate to this story . . . I share with you the best life advice that I always give to anyone who asks. In true teacher fashion, I composed this using a "1.a. and 1.b." model of expression. 1.a. for me is my Christian faith, as I am nothing without it, and it has proven to be the foundation of all that is good in my life. It has allowed me to redefine what it means to experience hardships and tragedy. As a good friend in ministry has said, "God doesn't give you what you can handle. He absolutely gives you more than you can handle so you can learn to depend on him." I encourage you, if you have already accepted Him into your heart, lean and press into that on the hard days, and if you have never considered that choice, I ask that you treat this as an invitation to do just that. But 1.b. is community, the intentional real community that you build around you as your support system and that will help insulate and carry you on your journey, whatever that journey may hold. Your community can consist of close family and friends, coworkers, neighbors, church family, or anyone else you know you can talk to who will listen without judgement and get their "hands dirty" with you. Although you may have strong faith, you also cannot do life alone; you must have a community to help sustain you, regardless of how big or small it may be, and for many of us, including myself, it may start with just one person. If you find that you are lacking community or struggling to build or find it wherever you might be, I encourage you to reach out to me, as I will always be willing to connect with anyone to share resources or just be a listening ear. When someone asks why I am willing to open myself up to the world like that, I am reminded that as was done for me, so should I do for someone else. I have never forgotten the kindnesses extended to me, but I also recall the words of Jesus echoing through time:

> *For I was hungry and you gave me food, I was thirsty and you gave me drink, I was a stranger and you welcomed me, I was naked and you clothed me, I was sick and you visited me, I was in prison and you came to me. Then the righteous will answer him, saying, "Lord, when did we see*

you hungry and feed you, or thirsty and give you a drink? And when did we see you a stranger and welcome you, or naked and clothe you? And when did we see you sick or in prison and visit you?" And the King will answer them, "Truly, I say to you, as you did it to one of the least of these my brothers, you did it to me." (Matt. 25:35-40, ESV)

acknowledgments

THERE ARE SO MANY amazing people who are responsible for helping me achieve this milestone, and I would like to do my best to thank even a fraction of them.

First, to the great staff at Ballast Books, who not only made this process easy and enjoyable but always treated me as if my story mattered.

To my son, Chris, who is the reason for me writing this book and the reason for me doing any of the advocacy work I've been blessed to do over the last ten years. He has made me a better man, husband, father, and person, and if I accomplish nothing else in this life, I am honored to call myself his dad.

To my wife, Faith, who has been my biggest fan and supporter, my partner in life and in ministry, and a travel companion who never complains about going to the next place we find ourselves doing ministry but embraces it with a love for the work that amazes.

Of course, a special thank you to my parents, Ted and Sandy Fela, whom I would frequently complain about or be disappointed in, especially in my youth, but who nonetheless taught me life's greatest lessons. My mother, while she had what I referred to as an "eccentric" nature, still demonstrated the importance and value of truly loving your family and accepting them despite their faults. She showed me that when you love someone, you will do anything for them without hesitation. My father, Ted, was a huge focus of this story. Despite his weaknesses as a husband and father, he loved my mother and me, showing it in the ways he could, even something as simple as "Don't Panic!"

To all my ministry and advocate friends around the country, especially those at Key Ministry, whom I thank for giving me a chance to be on a big stage years ago and without whom I probably would not have been given anywhere near the amount of opportunities I have had in this world. Even beyond the ways they gave just another dad a voice, I am honored to have so many of these incredible authors and speakers as not just professional acquaintances but also as real friends. So, to Steve Grcevich, Beth Golik, Sandra Peoples, Sarah Broady, Lamar Hardwick, Cindi and Joe Ferrini, Stephanie Holmes, Stephen Doc Hunsley, Jolene Philo, and so many more of you whom I don't have room to thank here, I owe you one when I see you. I also want to acknowledge those in the disability world who are putting a spotlight on the needs of fathers in this world and the specific ways they need to be supported. I thank my friend David Hirsch of Special Fathers Network, whose drive and passion to serve dads and men is nothing short of extraordinary. I am grateful for his mentoring and friendship over the years. I also want to thank so many of the other great advocates for men around the country, like my friends Steve Chatman, Todd Evans, and Dan Holmes, as well as so many of my local Chicago dads crew—you know who you are, so I won't embarrass you.

Finally, to my friend Wayne Messmer, who wrote the foreword to this book and played a special part in the ending of this story. Wayne taught me how to appreciate every moment of life because you don't know when it can be taken from you. He also reminded me that you don't always know the true value of a moment until it becomes a memory. My son, Chris, has inspired me to be a better man, but Wayne is the person who showed me how and who has been a constant example of how to show up in life, whether on a huge stage or through simply sharing a meal with a friend.